CASSEROLE COOKERY

CASSEROLE COOKERY

Rosemary Wadey

TESCO

NOTE

1. All recipes serve four unless otherwise stated.

2. All spoon measurements are level.

3. All eggs are sizes 3 and 4 unless otherwise stated.

4. Preparation times given are an average calculated during recipe testing.

5. Metric and imperial measurements have been calculated separately. Use one set of measurements only as they are not exact equivalents.

6. Cooking times may vary slightly depending on the individual oven. Dishes should be placed in the centre of the oven unless otherwise specified.

7. Always preheat the oven or grill to the specified temperature.

CONTENTS

This edition published in 1990
for Tesco Stores Ltd
Cheshunt, Herts, EN8 9SL
by Peerage Books,
81 Fulham Road, London SW3 6RB

© 1983 Peerage Books

Produced by Mandarin Offset
Printed and bound in Hong Kong

INTRODUCTION

A casserole is defined by my dictionary as a heatproof earthenware vessel in which food is cooked and served. The essential features are that it is heatproof and has a really tight-fitting lid. The dictionary term must, however, be sliding out of date for fewer casserole dishes are now being made of earthenware, although there is still something very attractive about these traditional brown dishes. Probably the most popular type today is the wide range of enamelled cast iron pots available in a variety of shapes, sizes, colours and patterns that look smart on the table. Other attractive dishes are made of pottery, heat-resistant glass, metal and china. Many have the added attraction of being dual-purpose for they are flameproof, meaning they can be used on the gas or electric hotplate as well as in the oven, so that the 'frying-off' process (see right) can be carried out in the actual casserole instead of in a frying pan. Some casseroles absorb the heat from the oven more quickly than others, in the same way they also cool more rapidly. The heavyweight casseroles obviously take a little longer to 'get going' but once they have heated up the cooking is intensified, thus making the cooking time in all types of pots more or less the same in the end.

Casserole cooking
The idea of casserole cooking is to produce a richly flavoured and perfectly tender dish of meat, poultry, game, fish or vegetables. The food is cooked in varying amounts of liquid, with the choice of a wide variety of other ingredients, in a tightly closed container (to prevent evaporation and loss of flavours) in a moderate to slow oven. The great advantage is that, apart from the preliminary preparation and perhaps the finishing off, most casseroles need little attention.

A casserole is, in fact, similar to a stew except that it is always cooked in the oven, whereas some stews are cooked entirely on the hob. The ingredients and the general cooking methods are similar. Stews are supposed to be for cooking the cheaper, tougher cuts of meat, but in fact these same cheap cuts will casserole beautifully, with delicious results, for often the best flavour is found in the cheaper parts of the carcass. However, there is no need to look upon the casserole as a culinary poor relation, for the French, who passed on to us the word (of Greek origin), are past masters of this method of cooking.

And even the best cuts of meat, such as steaks, fillet of beef and veal escalopes, can all be used to produce very special casseroles.

Diced or small pieces of meat, vegetables, fish and game are traditionally associated with casserole cooking, but, of course, pieces and quarters of poultry or game as well as all types of chops and cutlets — with or without bone — can be used. Whole joints of meat are most successful too, as are whole chickens, whole game birds and whole individual fish. The cooking times, in this case, are longer than for roasting but the flavours and juices produced make them worthwhile and tenderness is guaranteed; and of course other dishes can be cooked in the oven alongside the casserole.

Most of the recipes in the book serve four; but they are suitable to double up either for a larger party or to make an extra one for the freezer. With whole joints increase the cooking time proportionately. For other cuts of meat, the cooking time is the same as on the original recipe.

Frying-off
The cheaper the cut, the slower and longer the cooking should be; but it is advisable first of all to 'seal' the meat or poultry in hot fat. This 'frying-off' not only seals in the juices but keeps the shape of a joint or bird intact, giving it a far more attractive appearance when cooked. Vegetables, such as onions, are best fried-off, too, in order to aid digestion.

Slow cookers and pressure cookers
Many people find slow cookers and pressure cookers convenient and economical alternatives to oven-cooked casseroles. The slow cooker, after preliminary preparation, cooks the dish on a low heat, usually taking 6-8 hours or longer. The advantages are that once under way it needs no attention at all and the amount of electricity used is minimal; it is ideal for the extra busy housewife or for the business woman, who likes to come home to a ready-cooked evening meal. Small size cookers cater admirably for one or two persons.

A pressure cooker cuts cooking time because of the pressure built up inside the container, and many people become firmly attached to their pressure cookers once they are used to them.

With both types of cooker it is essential to read the

instructions carefully beforehand and then always to follow them closely whilst cooking; so that with only minor adjustments, made according to the manufacturers' instructions, most casserole recipes can be adapted for use with either.

Meat casseroles

This chapter covers all types of meat casseroles, showing that any meat—beef, lamb, pork, veal, bacon and ham, rabbit and even oxtail—can be turned into something special. Wines, sherry, Madeira, brandy and other types of alcohol are added to a number of the recipes to enhance the flavours and help to tenderize meat. Many old favourites appear, with plenty of new ideas; and for those who want even more scope, many of the recipes can form the filling for good pies—simply cool the casserole, transfer to a pie dish, cover with a pastry lid and cook.

Poultry and game casseroles

The poultry and game chapter presents a selection of exciting recipes suitable for entertaining. Because game is seasonal, some of the recipes can only be made at certain times, unless you buy the meat in season and then store in the freezer. Game is much easier to find now that supermarkets sell frozen oven-ready birds.

Fish casseroles

Fish may not spring to mind as a casserole ingredient, but I hope I have changed that concept, for fish lends itself so well to this method of cooking. Some of the fish used is everyday but some is more exotic and may not be easy to find in certain areas. Again larger supermarkets now stock wider varieties of fish and shellfish. Fish casseroles require shorter cooking because of the composition of the flesh but respond well to 'enclosed' cooking.

Flavours from abroad

As an interesting contrast to the traditional recipes included in the other chapters, this one presents special ideas from abroad. Here the French classics appear alongside dishes from Poland, Australia, New Zealand, America and Switzerland, among others. The ingredients used are often well known but used in surprising combinations.

Stock

A word about stock to use for casseroles. Obviously it is best to make your own; purchased stock cubes or powder are, however, a good substitute but watch the salt content, you may need to reduce the amount of salt added for seasoning. Similarly, a bouquet garni sachet can be bought ready-made but it is simple to prepare yourself: tie together in a piece of muslin 1 bay leaf, 2 sprigs of parsley, a sprig of thyme and a few black peppercorns. Remove it from the casserole before serving.

Freezing

A final note on freezing casseroles. While writing and testing recipes for this book I have frozen many of them successfully. Most are suitable, but watch out for those with a lot of cream or egg yolks in them, because they don't freeze well. And remember if the casserole is highly spiced, 2-3 weeks is long enough in the freezer; but the majority will freeze successfully for 2-3 months, apart from fish, for which 4 weeks is long enough. I prefer to thaw before reheating, either at room temperature or in a microwave oven; but casseroles can be reheated from frozen in a slow oven with occasional stirring. Reheating must be done thoroughly; once the contents have boiled, continue for 15-20 minutes. You can freeze the food in the casserole if you line it with foil, then remove the pack when frozen, thus releasing the dish. The same dish, if available, can then be used for reheating. Double thickness polythene bags, foil bags or polythene or foil containers are also suitable. Remember to leave a 2.5 cm (1 inch) headspace for liquids to expand during freezing.

Advance preparation

If preparing a casserole the day before you are going to serve it, cook the recipe for all but the last 20 minutes. The next day, cook the casserole for 45 minutes to 1 hour at a lower temperature and complete the finishing touches.

MEAT

Burgundy beef

2 tablespoons oil	salt
675 g (1½ lb) stewing steak, cut into strips about 5 × 2.5 cm (2 inches × 1 inch)	freshly ground black pepper
	100 g (4 oz) stoned prunes (soaked overnight if necessary – see instructions on packet)
2 onions, peeled and sliced	
1 garlic clove, peeled and crushed	1 tablespoon cornflour
450 ml (¾ pint) red wine	100 g (4 oz) button mushrooms, trimmed and halved
1 tablespoon tomato purée	To garnish:
1 bay leaf	bacon rolls
2 teaspoons Worcestershire sauce	sprigs of parsley (optional)

Preparation time: *15 minutes*
Cooking time: *2¼ hours*
Oven: *160°C, 325°F, Gas Mark 3*

1. Heat the oil in a flameproof casserole and fry the stewing steak until sealed. Add the onions and garlic and continue cooking for a few minutes, stirring frequently.
2. Add the wine and bring to the boil. Stir in the tomato purée, bay leaf, Worcestershire sauce, salt, pepper and prunes. Cover the casserole tightly.
3. Cook in a preheated oven for 2 hours.
4. Blend the cornflour with a little cold water and stir into the casserole with the mushrooms and a little extra stock if necessary. Discard the bay leaf and return the casserole to the oven for 15 minutes, until the mushrooms are cooked. Serve hot, garnished with bacon rolls and parsley (if using).

To make bacon rolls, first cut off the bacon rinds with a sharp knife or kitchen scissors and cut out any white gristle or bone. Stretch out evenly on a board using the back of a knife. This will make the bacon more even and easier to roll up. If you are worried about the rolls unwinding during cooking, thread several on to the metal skewers or push a wooden cocktail stick into each roll

Beef carbonnade

675 g (1½ lb) chuck or braising steak, cut into 4 cm (1½ inch) cubes	pinch of ground mace or nutmeg
	1 bay leaf
3 tablespoons flour	2 teaspoons brown sugar
salt	2 teaspoons vinegar
freshly ground black pepper	1½ teaspoons French mustard
4 tablespoons oil or dripping	3-4 carrots, peeled and cut into sticks
2 large onions, peeled and thinly sliced	
	100 g (4 oz) button mushrooms, trimmed
1-2 garlic cloves, peeled and crushed	chopped fresh parsley, to garnish (optional)
300 ml (½ pint) brown ale	
300 ml (½ pint) beef stock	
2 tablespoons tomato ketchup or 1 tablespoon tomato purée	

Preparation time: *15 minutes*
Cooking time: *about 1¾ hours*
Oven: *160°C, 325°F, Gas Mark 3*

1. Coat the meat with flour seasoned with salt and pepper. Heat 3 tablespoons of the oil or dripping in a pan and fry meat until browned. Transfer to a casserole.
2. Fry the onions and garlic in the same pan with the remaining oil added, until lightly coloured, then stir in the remaining seasoned flour and cook for 1 minute.
3. Gradually add the brown ale and stock and bring to the boil. Add the ketchup, mace, salt and pepper, bay leaf, sugar, vinegar and mustard and pour over the beef.
4. Add the carrots to the casserole, mix well, cover tightly and cook in a preheated oven for 1¼ hours.
5. Taste and adjust the seasoning, add the mushrooms and return to the oven for 25-30 minutes until quite tender. Discard the bay leaf and serve sprinkled with chopped parsley (if using).

TOP TO BOTTOM: Burgundy beef; Beef carbonnade

Boeuf à l'orange

3 tablespoons oil	300 ml (½ pint) beef stock
675 g (1½ lb) braising steak, cut into 2.5 cm (1 inch) cubes	2 oranges
	1 tablespoon tomato purée
225 g (8 oz) button onions, peeled	3 tablespoons brandy
	1 tablespoon black treacle
1 garlic clove, peeled and crushed	To garnish:
	sprigs of parsley
2 tablespoons flour	orange wedges or slices

Preparation time: *30 minutes*
Cooking time: *about 2½ hours*
Oven: *160°C, 325°F, Gas Mark 3*

1. Heat the oil in a pan and fry the meat until well sealed. Transfer to a casserole.
2. Fry the onions and garlic in the same fat until golden brown, then transfer to the casserole.
3. Stir the flour into the fat in the pan and cook for 1 minute. Gradually add the stock and bring to the boil.
4. Pare the rind thinly from the oranges with a potato peeler and cut into julienne strips. Add to the sauce with the juice from both oranges
5. Add the tomato purée, brandy and black treacle to the sauce and add salt and pepper. Pour over the beef and cover the casserole tightly.
6. Cook in a preheated oven for about 2 hours.
7. Add the mushrooms, adjust the seasoning and add a little extra stock if necessary. Return to the oven for about 30 minutes or until tender.
8. Serve garnished with parsley sprigs and pieces of orange.

CLOCKWISE FROM THE BOTTOM: Fillet of beef Dijon; Boeuf à l'orange; Masterton beef

Masterton beef

1 kg (2 lb) braising steak, trimmed and cut into 8 even-sized pieces	2 tablespoons flour
	150 ml (¼ pint) red wine
	150 ml (¼ pint) beef stock
salt	1 × 425 g (15 oz) can tomatoes
freshly ground black pepper	1 tablespoon tomato purée
2 tablespoons oil or dripping	2 tablespoons capers
2 onions, peeled and sliced	1 tablespoon wine vinegar
1 garlic clove, peeled and crushed	sprig of parsley, to garnish (optional)

Preparation time: *15 minutes*
Cooking time: *2-2½ hours*
Oven: *180°C, 350°F, Gas Mark 4*

1. Sprinkle the meat with salt and pepper. Heat 1 tablespoon of the oil in a pan and fry the beef until well sealed all over. Transfer to a casserole.
2. Add the remaining oil to the pan and fry the onions and garlic until lightly browned.
3. Stir in the flour and cook for 1 minute, then gradually add the wine, stock and juice from the tomatoes and bring to the boil for 2 minutes. Add the tomato purée, capers, vinegar and salt and pepper, then pour over the beef and add the tomatoes.
4. Cover the casserole and cook in a preheated oven for 2-2½ hours or until tender. Taste and adjust the seasoning.
5. Serve garnished with parsley (if using).

Variation:
Pieces of pie veal make a good alternative to the beef in this recipe. To change the flavour of this casserole, omit the capers and in their place add 100 g (4 oz) no-need-to-soak dried apricots. To turn it into a hotpot, put the prepared ingredients into a shallow casserole and cover with a layer of thinly sliced potatoes — allowing about 675 g (1½ lb). Brush with melted butter and cook uncovered for about 2 hours until the meat is tender and potatoes browned and crispy.

Fillet of beef Dijon

675-750 g (1½-1¾ lb) piece fillet of beef	2 tablespoons brandy
	6 tablespoons single cream
salt	2 teaspoons cornflour
freshly ground black pepper	1 tablespoon finely chopped gherkins (optional)
25 g (1 oz) butter or margarine	
juice of 1 orange	To garnish:
1 tablespoon lemon juice	fried button mushrooms
4 tablespoons beef stock	fried bread crescents
1-2 tablespoons wine vinegar	sprigs of parsley
1 tablespoon Dijon mustard	

Preparation time: *10 minutes*
Cooking time: *50 minutes*
Oven: *200°C, 400°F, Gas Mark 6*

Ask the butcher for the thick end of the fillet of beef (the rump end) and a thin piece of fat the same size as the steak to keep it really moist during cooking.

1. Trim the beef and sprinkle well with salt and pepper. If using a piece of fat as suggested, tie it evenly around the piece of beef with string.
2. Melt the butter in a pan and fry the joint all over until evenly browned. Transfer to a casserole.
3. Add the fruit juices, stock and the vinegar, according to taste, to the pan drippings and bring to the boil. Add salt and pepper and pour the mixture over the beef. Cover the casserole tightly.
4. Cook in a preheated oven for 35 minutes, basting once during cooking. For well cooked beef increase the cooking time by 10-15 minutes.
5. Transfer the joint to a serving plate and keep warm. Remove the string and take off the fat if preferred.
6. Transfer the casserole juices to a saucepan (unless using a flameproof casserole) and bring back to the boil. Add the mustard and brandy, then blend the cream and cornflour together and add to the sauce. Bring slowly back to the boil, adjust the seasoning and add the gherkins (if using).
7. Garnish the joint with fried mushrooms, bread crescents and parsley. Serve the beef cut into fairly thick slices, with the sauce.

Beery beef

Serves 4-6

1 × 1.5 kg (3 lb) joint of silverside or topside of beef	2 bay leaves
450 ml (¾ pint) pale ale	1 tablespoon demerara sugar
1 tablespoon oil or dripping	6 whole cloves
2 onions, peeled and sliced	4 carrots, peeled and quartered
1 garlic clove, peeled and crushed	2 turnips, peeled and thickly sliced
salt	1 tablespoon cornflour
freshly ground black pepper	chopped fresh parsley, to garnish

Preparation time: *20 minutes, plus marinating overnight*
Cooking time: *about 1½ - 1¾ hours*
Oven: *180°C, 350°F, Gas Mark 4*

1. Place the joint in a casserole or basin just large enough to hold it and pour the pale ale over. Cover and leave to marinate for at least 24 hours (and up to 48 hours), turning several times.
2. Drain the joint and wipe dry. Heat the oil or dripping in a pan and fry the meat to brown all over. Transfer to a larger casserole.
3. Fry the onions and garlic in the same fat until lightly browned, drain off any excess fat from the pan, add the marinade and bring to the boil.
4. Add salt and pepper, bay leaves, sugar and cloves and pour over the joint. Cover tightly and cook in a preheated oven for 45 minutes.
5. Add the carrots and turnips to the casserole, baste the joint and replace the lid. Return to the oven for ¾-1 hour or until the meat is tender.
6. Drain off all the juices to a saucepan and skim off any fat. Blend the cornflour with a little cold water and add to the sauce. Bring to the boil for 1 minute, adjust the seasoning and pour into a jug.
7. Serve the meat on a warmed plate surrounded by the vegetables, sprinkled with parsley, and the sauce. The leftovers of this joint are excellent served cold with salads.

Variation:

Cubes of braising or chuck steak can be used for this casserole. Allow about 1 kg (2 lb), cut into 5 cm (2 inches) pieces and marinate in the ale as for a joint. All casseroles made with beer are better still if made the day before required and reheated for about an hour when needed. If using cubes of beef, make as above, allowing about 2 hours in the oven and when the juices have been thickened, pour back over the meat before serving.

Beef olives with pecan nuts

4 thin slices topside of beef, beaten	1 tablespoon chopped fresh parsley
1 tablespoon oil	40 g (1½ oz) shelled pecan nuts, chopped
25 g (1 oz) butter or margarine	freshly ground black pepper
2 tablespoons flour	a little ground coriand﹖
300 ml (½ pint) beef stock	1 egg, beaten
Stuffing:	To garnish:
40 g (1½ oz) long-grain rice	4 tablespoons sour﹖
salt	few pecan halves
25 g (1 oz) butter or margarine	chopped fresh pars﹖
1 onion, peeled and chopped	
½ teaspoon dried thyme	

Preparation time: *20 minutes*
Cooking time: *about 1¼ hours*
Oven: *180°C, 350°F, Gas Mark 4*

Beef olives are made from slices of beef taken of﹖ joint. They need to be beaten between 2 sheets ﹖ or damp greaseproof paper to give them their ch﹖ tic thinness.

1. For the stuffing, cook the rice in boiling salted ﹖ 12-14 minutes or until tender. Drain well.
2. Melt the fat in a pan and fry the onion gently﹖ Add the thyme, parsley, pecan nuts, salt, pepper, ﹖ and cooked rice and bind with the egg — the mixtu﹖ be fairly slack.
3. Divide the stuffing between the beef slices, sp﹖ over part of the meat, then roll up carefully to en﹖ secure with wooden cocktail sticks.
4. Heat the oil and fat in a frying pan and fry the ﹖ until browned. Transfer to a shallow casserole.
5. Stir the flour into the pan juices and cook f﹖ Gradually add the stock and sherry and bring to﹖
6. Add salt and pepper and strain the sauce ove﹖ Cover with foil or a lid and cook in a preheate﹖ about 1¼ hours or until tender.
7. Remove the cocktail sticks and serve each oli﹖ with a spoonful of soured cream, a few pecan h﹖ sprinkled with chopped parsley.

Gladstone hotpot

2 tablespoons oil or dripping	*2 tablespoons flour*
675 g (1½ lb) braising steak, cut into 4 × 1 cm (1½ × ½ inch) strips	*300 ml (½ pint) beef stock*
	1 tablespoon French mustard
	1 tablespoon Worcestershire sauce
2 large onions, peeled and sliced	*1 tablespoon soy sauce*
225 g (8 oz) carrots, peeled and sliced	*salt*
	freshly ground black pepper
1 green pepper, deseeded and sliced	*675 g (1½ lb) potatoes, peeled and sliced*
1 × 425 g (15 oz) can tomatoes	

Preparation time: *30 minutes*
Cooking time: *2¼ hours*
Oven: *180°C, 350°F, Gas Mark 4;*
         200°C, 400°F, Gas Mark 6

1. Heat the oil or dripping in a pan and fry the steak until well sealed. Remove from the pan.

2. Fry the onions in the same fat until golden brown and remove from the pan.
3. Layer the meat in a casserole with the onions, carrots, pepper and tomatoes drained from the juice.
4. Stir the flour into the fat in the pan and cook for 1 minute. Gradually add the stock and tomato juice and bring to the boil. Stir in the mustard, Worcestershire sauce, soy sauce, salt and pepper.
5. Pour over the contents of the casserole and cover with a thick layer of sliced potatoes.
6. Cover the casserole and cook in a preheated oven for 1½ hours.
7. Remove the lid from the casserole, increase the oven temperature and return to the oven for about 45 minutes or until the potatoes are golden brown.

LEFT TO RIGHT: Beef olives with pecan nuts; Gladstone hotpot

Devilled meatballs

550 g (1¼ lb) raw minced beef
40 g (1½ oz) fresh
breadcrumbs
1 small onion, peeled and finely
chopped
salt
freshly ground black pepper
1 tablespoon Worcestershire
sauce
2 tablespoons oil
225 g (8 oz) carrots, peeled
and cut into thin sticks
1 large cooking apple, peeled,
cored and diced

Sauce:
1 tablespoon flour
1½ teaspoons dry mustard
1½ teaspoon Dijon mustard
1 tablespoon soy sauce
1 tablespoon Worcestershire
sauce
1 tablespoon sweet chutney
300 ml (½ pint) beef stock
watercress or parsley, to
garnish

Preparation time: *20 minutes*
Cooking time: *45 minutes*
Oven: *180°C, 350°F, Gas Mark 4*

1. Mix the minced beef thoroughly with the breadcrumbs, onion, salt, pepper and Worcestershire sauce. Divide into 16 and shape into balls.

2. Heat the oil in a pan and fry the meatballs gently until browned. Remove from the pan and pour off all but 1 tablespoon of the fat.
3. To make the sauce, stir the flour and dry mustard into the residue in the pan followed by the Dijon mustard, soy sauce, Worcestershire sauce, chutney and stock. Bring to the boil and add salt and pepper.
4. Lay the carrots and apples in a casserole and arrange the meatballs on top. Pour the sauce over and cover the casserole. Cook in a preheated oven for about 45 minutes.
5. Uncover the casserole, remove any fat from the surface and stir lightly. Garnish with watercress or parsley. Spaghetti or noodles make a good accompaniment.

LEFT TO RIGHT: Devilled meatballs; Beef and horseradish

Hot spiced beef

2 tablespoons oil or dripping	1 × 425 g (15 oz) can peeled
675 g (1½ lb) good stewing	tomatoes
steak, trimmed and cut into 2.5	1 tablespoon wine vinegar
cm (1 inch) cubes	2 tablespoons apricot jam
3 large onions, peeled	150 ml (¼ pint) beef stock
1 × 200 g (7 oz) can	salt
unsweetened pineapple rings	freshly ground black pepper
2 teaspoons curry powder	chopped fresh parsley, to
1 tablespoon tomato purée	garnish

Preparation time: *15 minutes*
Cooking time: *2½ hours*
Oven: *160°C, 325°F, Gas Mark 3*

This recipe has a very mild curry taste suitable even for those who dislike curry. Lamb, pork or any kind of poultry can be used instead of beef. Use boned shoulder of lamb or boned hand or shoulder of pork and cut the cooking time to 1½-1¾ hours. If using chicken, use 12 drumsticks or 4 portions cut in half. Turkey casserole meat or boneless thigh meat is

also suitable and these only need 1-1¼ hours cooking. This dish is also good served with boiled rice mixed with peppers, chopped toasted nuts, raisins and peas.

1. Heat the oil in a pan and fry the beef until evenly browned. Transfer to a casserole.
2. Chop the onions and pineapple very finely, preferably in a food processor, then add to the pan with all the other ingredients, including the pineapple juice, and bring to the boil. Pour over the beef, mix well and cover the casserole tightly.
3. Cook in a preheated oven for 2½ hours or until the meat is tender. Taste and adjust the seasoning.
4. Garnish with plenty of chopped fresh parsley. Serve with plain boiled rice or creamed potatoes.

Beef and horseradish

675 g (1½ lb) braising steak,	25 g (1 oz) flour
trimmed and cut into 4 portions	600 ml (1 pint) beef stock
salt	1 tablespoon Worcestershire
freshly ground black pepper	sauce
1 teaspoon ground coriander	2 tablespoons double cream
1 teaspoon ground ginger	3-4 tablespoons creamed
2 tablespoons oil or dripping	horseradish
16 pickling onions, peeled	celery leaves, to garnish
3 sticks celery, sliced	

Preparation time: *15 minutes*
Cooking time: *about 2½ hours*
Oven: *160°C, 325°F, Gas Mark 3*

1. Sprinkle the meat with salt and pepper and rub in with the coriander and ginger. Heat the oil in a pan and fry until sealed all over, then place in a shallow casserole.
2. Fry the onions until brown and celery until soft in the same fat. Stir in the flour, cook for 1 minute, then gradually add the stock and bring to the boil. Add salt, pepper and the Worcestershire sauce and pour over the beef.
3. Cover and cook in a preheated oven for 2 hours.
4. Stir in the cream and the horseradish and return to the oven for 45 minutes; garnish with celery leaves.

Gingered beef

675g (1½ lb) braising steak, trimmed and cut into 2.5 cm (1 inch) cubes	*2 onions, peeled and sliced*
50 (2 oz) flour	*300 ml (½ pint) beef stock*
salt	*1 × 225g (8 oz) can tomatoes*
freshly ground black pepper	*2 tablespoons vinegar*
1½-2 teaspoons ground ginger	*1 tablespoon thick honey*
3 tablespoons oil or dripping	*1 tablespoon Worcestershire sauce*
1 tablespoon grated root ginger	*1 × 425g (15 oz) can red kidney beans or cannellini beans, drained*
1 garlic clove, peeled and crushed	

Preparation time: *30 minutes*
Cooking time: *about 2¼ hours*
Oven: *160°C, 325°F, Gas Mark 3*

This casserole has a rich tangy flavour which soon becomes a firm favourite particularly because it is also easy to prepare and cook. It can be cooked in bulk and freezes well for up to 2 months — no longer because of its spiciness. Cook as far as adding the beans but do not add them. Cool the casserole rapidly and pack into foil containers or bags, solid plastic containers or thick polythene bags standing in a bowl to keep a good shape. Alternatively line a casserole with foil, add the mixture and freeze until solid, then remove and wrap and return to the freezer leaving the casserole ready for use again. Remember anything containing liquid will expand during freezing, so always allow at least a 2.5 cm (1 inch) headspace, to prevent the container or bag exploding during storage. Thaw or part thaw before cooking and add the beans when quite liquid. Cook for 1 hour in a moderate oven (180°C, 350°F, Gas Mark 4).

1. Coat the meat with flour seasoned with salt, pepper and ground ginger.
2. Heat the oil or dripping in a pan and fry the meat to seal. Transfer to a casserole. Fry the root ginger, garlic and onions in the same fat until light browned, then stir in the remaining seasoned flour and cook for 1 minute.
3. Gradually add the stock, tomatoes, vinegar, honey and Worcestershire sauce, with salt and pepper to taste. Bring to the boil. Pour over the beef, cover the casserole and cook in a preheated oven for about 1¾ hours or until almost tender.
4. Add the beans and stir through the casserole. Adjust the seasoning, replace the lid and return to the oven for 20-25 minutes. Serve with jacket potatoes and a salad.

Beef noodle casserole

Serves 4-5

175g (6 oz) green noodles	*1 tablespoon tomato purée*
675g (1½ lb) raw minced beef	*1 teaspoon dried oregano*
2 onions, peeled and chopped	*salt*
1-2 garlic cloves, peeled and crushed	*freshly ground black pepper*
2 teaspoons cornflour	*25g (1 oz)*
1 × 425g (15 oz) can tomatoes	*25g (1 oz)*
150 ml (¼ pint) beef stock	*300 ml (½*
1 tablespoon soy sauce	*40-50g (1*
1 tablespoon Worcestershire sauce	*Cheddar ch*

Preparation time: *20 minutes*
Cooking time: *25-30 minutes*
Oven: *200°C, 400°F, Gas Mark 6*

1. Cook the noodles in boiling salted wat until partly cooked. Drain.
2. Cook the minced beef gently in a pan until browned, stirring frequently. Add the and continue cooking for 3-4 minutes.
3. Blend the cornflour with some of the tomatoes, then stir into the beef with the soy sauce, Worcestershire sauce, tomato salt and pepper. Bring to the boil and cook
4. Put half the noodles in the base of a casse the meat mixture, then add the rest of the no
5. Melt the butter in a pan, stir in the flour minute, then gradually add the milk and bri 1 minute. Add salt and pepper and pour ove
6. Sprinkle over the cheese, cover and heated oven for 15 minutes, then uncove cooking for a further 10-15 minutes or until brown and crispy.

Variation:
100 g (4 oz) sliced mushrooms may be adde Plain noodles may be used in place of green n wholemeal ones.

Angostura mince cobbler

550 g (1 ¼ lb) raw minced beef	Scone topping:
1 large onion, peeled and sliced	*175 g (6 oz) self-raising flour*
2 carrots, peeled and diced	*40 g (1 ½ oz) butter or margarine*
300 ml (½ pint) beef stock	*salt*
1 ½ tablespoons Angostura bitters	*freshly ground black pepper*
1 tablespoon tomato purée	*½ teaspoon dried mixed herbs*
salt	*1 egg, beaten*
freshly ground black pepper	*about 2 tablespoons milk*
2 teaspoons cornflour	*few sesame seeds (optional)*

Preparation time: *20 minutes*
Cooking time: *40 minutes*
Oven: *180°C, 350°F, Gas Mark 4;*
200°C, 400°F, Gas Mark 6

1. Fry the beef gently in a pan with no extra fat until the juices begin to run, stirring frequently. Add the onion and carrots and continue cooking for a few minutes.
2. Add the stock, Angostura bitters, tomato purée, salt and pepper and bring to the boil. Blend the cornflour in a little cold water, add to the pan and cook until thickened.
3. Turn into a casserole, cover and cook in a preheated oven for 20 minutes.
4. For the scone topping, sift the flour into a bowl and rub in the fat until the mixture resembles fine breadcrumbs. Add salt and pepper and stir in the herbs. Bind together with egg and sufficient milk to give a softish dough.
5. Pat out the dough on a floured surface to about 1 cm (½ inch) thick and cut into 4 cm (1½ inch) rounds.
6. Remove the casserole from the oven. Increase the oven temperature. Arrange the scones in an overlapping circle around the top of the casserole. Brush with milk and sprinkle with sesame seeds (if using).
7. Return the casserole to the oven and bake uncovered for about 20 minutes or until the scones are well risen and golden brown. Serve at once.

Variation:
Minced pork or veal may be used in place of the beef.

TOP TO BOTTOM: Beef noodle casserole; Angostura mince cobbler

Cidered lamb with dumplings

8 middle neck lamb chops or about 1 kg (2 lb) stewing lamb	150 ml (¼ pint) beef stock
salt	300 ml (½ pint) cider
freshly ground black pepper	1 teaspoon mixed herbs
1 tablespoon oil or dripping	1 aubergine, trimmed and chopped
1 onion, peeled and sliced	Dumplings:
1 garlic clove, peeled and crushed	100 g (4 oz) self-raising flour
1 red pepper, deseeded and sliced	pinch of salt
	50 g (2 oz) shredded suet
1 tablespoon plain flour	1 teaspoon dried mixed herbs

Preparation time: *15 minutes*
Cooking time: *about 1½ hours*
Oven: *180°C, 350°F, Gas Mark 4*

1. Trim the lamb and sprinkle lightly with salt and pepper. Heat the oil or dripping in a pan and fry the lamb to brown all over. Transfer to a casserole.
2. Fry the onion, garlic and pepper in the same fat for a few minutes until soft.
3. Stir in the flour, cook for 1 minute, then gradually add the stock and cider and bring to the boil for 2 minutes.
4. Season well, add the mixed herbs and aubergine and pour over the lamb. Cover the casserole and cook in a preheated oven for about 1 hour or until almost tender.
5. Meanwhile, to make the dumplings, mix together the flour, salt, suet and herbs. Add sufficient cold water to make a soft dough. Shape into 8 balls.
6. Skim off any excess fat from the surface of the casserole, then add the dumplings. Replace the lid and continue to cook for 25-30 minutes or until the dumplings are cooked.

Apricot lamb

4 butterfly lamb chops (double loin chops)	150 ml (¼ pint) beef stock
salt	1 tablespoon paprika
freshly ground black pepper	75 g (3 oz) dried apricots, soaked overnight
1 tablespoon oil	sprigs of mint or parsley, to garnish
1 onion, peeled and chopped	
juice of 1 orange	

Preparation time: *10 minutes, plus overnight soaking*
Cooking time: *about 40 minutes*
Oven: *180°C, 350°F, Gas Mark 4*

Not all butchers sell butterfly chops; if they are not available use large thick chump or loin chops.

1. Trim the chops and sprinkle well with salt and pepper. Heat the oil in a pan and fry the chops until evenly browned. Transfer to a shallow casserole.
2. Fry the onion gently in the same fat until soft. Add the orange juice, stock, salt and pepper to taste and paprika. Simmer for 2 minutes.
3. Arrange the apricots around the chops, then pour over the sauce and cover the casserole.
4. Cook in a preheated oven for about 40 minutes until tender. Serve garnished with sprigs of mint or parsley.

Variation:
Canned apricots can be used in place of the dried ones. Allow 1 × 200 g (7oz) can apricot halves and replace 4 tablespoons stock with apricot juice; continue as above. This recipe can also be varied by using prunes in place of apricots. Use the no-need-to-soak variety now available, increase the amount to 150 g (5 oz) and cook in the same way as above. Serve with Duchesse potatoes; beat mashed potatoes with beaten egg until really smooth. Put into a piping bag fitted with a star nozzle and pipe whirls of potato on to greased baking sheets. Put into the oven above the casserole for about 30 minutes or until lightly browned. Alternatively brown the potatoes under a moderate grill.

TOP TO BOTTOM: Cidered lamb with dumplings; Apricot lamb

Orange lamb with rice

2 oranges	50 g (2 oz) raisins
675 g (1½ lb) lean boneless lamb, cut into 2.5 cm (1 inch) cubes	1 garlic clove, peeled and crushed
salt	¼ teaspoon ground coriander
freshly ground black pepper	175 g (6 oz) long-grain rice
1 tablespoon oil	To garnish
1 large onion, peeled and sliced	40 g (1½ oz) toasted almond slivers
450 ml (¾ pint) beef stock	orange twists
	watercress

Preparation time: *15 minutes*
Cooking time: *1 hour*
Oven: *180°C, 350°F, Gas Mark 4*

Choose shoulder meat, leg meat or lamb fillet for this recipe as they are the leanest cuts.

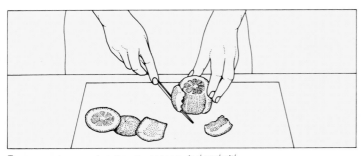

To ease out segments cut away orange rind and pith.

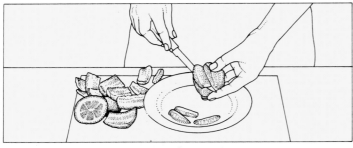

Cut between segments; ease segments from membrane.

1. Pare the rind finely from 1 orange, using a potato peeler, then cut into julienne strips. Cut away the white pith from the orange and ease away segments from between the membranes. Squeeze the juice from the second orange.
2. Sprinkle the lamb lightly with salt and pepper.
3. Heat the oil in a pan and fry the lamb until well sealed and lightly browned; remove from the pan.
4. Fry the onion in the same pan until lightly browned, then add the orange rind, segments and juice, the stock and raisins and bring to the boil. Add salt and pepper, garlic and coriander.

5. Place the rice in a lightly greased ovenproof dish, add the onion mixture and mix well. Lay the meat on top and cover with foil or a lid.
6. Cook in a preheated oven for 1 hour.
7. Remove the foil or lid, lightly mix the rice and meat together and sprinkle over the nuts. Garnish with orange twists and watercress.

Sago lamb

4 butterfly lamb chops (double loin chops)	4 tablespoons medium sherry
	2 tablespoons sago
salt	1 tablespoon tomato purée
freshly ground black pepper	1 teaspoon Worcestershire sauce
1 tablespoon oil	
2 onions, peeled and sliced	4 tomatoes, peeled and quartered
1 garlic clove, peeled and crushed	green or red pepper rings, to garnish
450 ml (¾ pint) beef stock	

Preparation time: *10 minutes*
Cooking time: *1¼ hours*
Oven: Oven: *180°C, 350°F, Gas Mark 4*

1. Sprinkle chops with salt and pepper. Heat the oil in a pan and fry the chops until well browned all over. Transfer to a shallow casserole, keeping the chops in a single layer.
2. Pour off all but 1 tablespoon of fat from the pan, then fry the onions and garlic until lightly browned.
3. Add the stock and sherry and bring to the boil. Stir in the sago, tomato purée, Worcestershire sauce and tomatoes and season with salt and pepper. Pour over the lamb and cover the casserole. Cook in a preheated oven for 1¼ hours.
4. Spoon any fat from the surface of the casserole, stir gently and garnish with green or red pepper.

Lamb and dill hotpot

2 tablespoons oil or dripping	salt
1.25 kg (2½ lb) scrag end neck of lamb, chopped	freshly ground black pepper
	1-1½ teaspoons dried
2 onions, peeled and sliced	dillweed
2 carrots, peeled and sliced	675 g (1½ lb) potatoes, peeled
1 tablespoon flour	and thinly sliced
150 ml (¼ pint) white wine	15 g (½ oz) melted butter or
300 ml (½ pint) beef stock	margarine
1 tablespoon tomato purée	
1 tablespoon demerara sugar	

Preparation time: *15 minutes*
Cooking time: *about 2 hours*
Oven: *180°C, 350°F, Gas Mark 4;*
200°C, 400°F, Gas Mark 6

Dill has a strong distinctive flavour; if you prefer a more definite taste of dill use the larger amount.

1. Heat the oil in a pan and fry the pieces of lamb until well browned, then place in a large casserole.
2. Fry the onions and carrots in the same fat for 2 minutes, then stir in the flour and cook for 1 minute. Gradually add the wine and stock and bring to the boil, stirring frequently.
3. Add the tomato purée, sugar, salt and pepper and the dillweed and pour into the casserole. Mix well with the lamb and level the top.
4. Arrange the sliced potatoes evenly over the contents of the casserole and brush the top layer with melted fat. Cover with a lid or foil.
5. Cook in a preheated oven for 1¼ hours. Increase the oven temperature, remove the foil from the casserole and return to the oven for about 30 minutes or until the potatoes are golden brown.

LEFT TO RIGHT: Orange lamb with rice; Lamb and dill hotpot

Pot roast leg of lamb with garlic and rosemary

Serves 6

1 leg of lamb, about 1.75 kg (4 lb)	300 ml (½ pint) beef stock
3-4 garlic cloves, peeled and cut into spikes	salt
	freshly ground black pepper
few sprigs of fresh rosemary or 1 tablespoon dried rosemary	900 g (2 lb) potatoes, peeled and diced
350 g (12 oz) pickling onions, peeled	fresh sprigs of rosemary, to garnish

Preparation time: *15 minutes*
Cooking time: *about 2 hours*
Oven: *190°C, 375°F, Gas Mark 5*

1. Wipe the lamb all over, then make deep cuts over the surface of the skin into the flesh.
2. Stick the garlic spikes and small pieces of rosemary into the cuts in the meat. If dried rosemary is used, sprinkle it over the skin after spiking with garlic.
3. Place the joint in a roasting tin and arrange the onions around it.
4. Bring the stock to the boil, add salt and pepper and pour over the lamb. Cover with foil and cook in a preheated oven for 1 hour.
5. Remove the foil, baste the joint and sprinkle the skin with salt and pepper. Arrange the diced potatoes around the lamb with the onions.
6. Return to the oven, covered with foil, and cook for 45 minutes. Baste the joint again and return to the oven uncovered for 15-20 minutes or until the meat is tender and the potatoes are cooked. Serve garnished with fresh rosemary.

Crisped loin of lamb

1 loin of lamb, about 1.25-1.5 kg (2½-3 lb), chined or chopped	150 ml (¼ pint) beef stock
	1-2 tablespoons wine vinegar
salt	Topping:
freshly ground black pepper	50 g (2 oz) fresh breadcrumbs
1 tablespoon oil or dripping	1 tablespoon chopped fresh mint or 2 teaspoons dried chopped mint
1 onion, peeled and diced	
2 carrots, peeled and diced	
1-2 leeks, trimmed and sliced	sprigs of fresh mint or parsley, to garnish

Preparation time: *15 minutes*
Cooking time: *1¾-2 hours*
Oven: *180°C, 350°F, Gas Mark 4;*
200°C, 400°F, Gas Mark 6

1. Trim the lamb and sprinkle lightly with salt and pepper. Heat the oil in a frying pan, then add the lamb and fry evenly to seal the meat. Remove from the pan.
2. Fry the onion and carrots gently in the same pan until beginning to soften, then transfer to a casserole with the leeks.
3. Place the lamb joint on the vegetables and add the stock, vinegar and salt and pepper.
4. Cover the casserole and cook in a preheated oven for 1¼ hours.
5. Remove the lid or foil and baste the joint. Combine the breadcrumbs, mint, salt and pepper and spoon over the fat.
6. Increase the oven temperature and return to the oven for about 30 minutes or until the topping is crisp and lightly browned and the lamb tender.
7. Serve the lamb cut into slices, or as a whole joint, surrounded by the vegetables and garnished with fresh mint or parsley. Serve the juices in a small jug.

A loin of lamb must be chopped or chined to make carving into chops possible. To chop, the whole joint is chopped through from the underneath so that the cooked chops will separate easily when cut. Chining means to remove or loosen the chine bone or the back bone attached to the chops. If loosened it can be removed easily once the joint is cooked; if taken off before cooking the meat will shrink badly from the bones and look unattractive.

Noisettes of lamb with fennel au gratin

4 thick noisettes of lamb	2 teaspoons cornflour
salt	40 g (1½ oz) fresh breadcrumbs
freshly ground black pepper	
2 teaspoons ground coriander	25 g (1 oz) mature Cheddar cheese, grated
1 tablespoon oil or dripping	
1 onion, peeled and thinly sliced	1 tablespoon grated Parmesan cheese
2 bulbs fennel, trimmed and chopped	fresh sprigs of fennel or parsley, to garnish
300 ml (½ pint) beef stock	

Preparation time: *20 minutes*
Cooking time: *about 1 hour 10 minutes*
Oven: *180°C, 350°F, Gas Mark 4*

Noisettes are boned loin chops tied into rounds. Sometimes they have kidney in the centre and are then known as kidney cutlets. If the noisettes are small or thin allow 2 per portion and cut the cooking time by 5-10 minutes.

1. Sprinkle the noisettes with salt, pepper and coriander. Heat the oil or dripping in a pan and fry the noisettes quickly to seal each side. Remove from the pan.
2. Fry the onion until soft in the same fat, then drain off any excess fat from the pan.
3. Place the onions and fennel in a casserole and lay the noisettes on the vegetables.
4. Pour the stock into a pan, add salt and pepper and bring to the boil. Pour over the meat and vegetables. Cover with a lid or foil.
5. Cook in a preheated oven for 45-50 minutes or until tender—the fennel should not be too soft.
6. Strain off the juices into a separate saucepan and spoon off any fat from the surface. Blend the cornflour with a little cold water, stir into the juices and bring to the boil, stirring until thickened. Adjust the seasoning and pour back over the vegetables and lamb.
7. Combine the breadcrumbs and cheeses and sprinkle over the noisettes. Place under a preheated moderate grill until the topping is golden brown and crisp. Garnish with sprigs of fennel or parsley

Variation:
Thick lamb chump chops or the double loin chops known as 'butterfly chops' may be used in place of noisettes. Trim off excess fat and proceed as above. Fennel is an acquired taste; if preferred it can be replaced with a mixture of sliced onions, potatoes and apples. Use 2 onions, 450 g (1 lb) potatoes and 2 eating apples.

CLOCKWISE FROM THE BOTTOM: Crisped loin of lamb; Pot roast leg of lamb with rosemary; Noisettes of lamb with fennel au gratin

Lamb lasagne

6 sheets green lasagne	6 tablespoons soured cream
salt	50 g (2 oz) mature Cheddar
1 tablespoon oil	cheese, grated
450 g (1 lb) raw minced lamb	1 tablespoon grated Parmesan
1 large onion, peeled and	cheese
chopped	To garnish:
2 carrots, peeled and chopped	tomato slices
1 × 425 g (15 oz) can tomatoes	cucumber slices
150 ml (¼ pint) beef stock	sprigs of parsley
1 tablespoon tomato purée	
freshly ground black pepper	
1 tablespoon chopped fresh	
mint or 1½ teaspoon dried mint	

Preparation time: *25 minutes*
Cooking time: *about 45 minutes*
Oven: *190°C, 375°F, Gas Mark 5*

1. Cook the lasagne, a few sheets at a time, in boiling salted water with the oil added for about 10 minutes or until just tender. Drain on paper towels.
2. Fry the lamb gently in a pan with no extra fat added, until sealed. Add the onion and carrots and continue cooking for 2 minutes.
3. Add the tomatoes, stock, tomato purée, salt, pepper and mint and bring to the boil. Simmer uncovered for 10 minutes until thickened. Adjust the seasoning.
4. Place a layer of lasagne in a greased ovenproof dish. Cover with half the meat mixture. Repeat the layers of lasagne and meat, ending with lasagne.
5. Spread the soured cream over the lasagne and sprinkle with a mixture of Cheddar or Parmesan cheese.
6. Cook in a preheated oven for about 45 minutes or until golden brown and bubbling. Garnish with tomato and cucumber slices and parsley.

Variation:
Use raw minced beef instead of the lamb, replace the mint with oregano or marjoram and add 100 g (4 oz) chopped mushrooms with the tomatoes.

Fillets of lamb Marsala

Serves 4-6

3 fillets of lamb, about 1 kg (2 lb)	grated rind of ½ lemon
salt	1 egg, beaten
freshly ground black pepper	25 g (1 oz) flour
50 g (2 oz) butter or margarine	300 ml (½ pint) beef stock
1 onion, peeled and finely chopped	4 tablespoons Marsala
	2 tablespoons lemon juice
1 stick celery, finely chopped	To garnish:
75 g (3 oz) fresh breadcrumbs	celery leaves
40 g (1½ oz) toasted almonds, chopped	25 g (1 oz) flaked almonds, toasted

Preparation time: *20 minutes*
Cooking time: *1½-2 hours*
30°C, 350°F, Gas Mark 4

the lamb and flatten a little if necessary. Sprinkle
with salt and pepper.
25 g (1 oz) of the butter in a frying pan and fry the
and celery until soft. Add to the breadcrumbs with the

nuts, lemon rind, salt and pepper and the egg. Stir to bind together.

3. Spread half the stuffing over one piece of lamb, cover with the second piece of lamb, then the remaining stuffing and finally the last fillet of lamb. Tie together with string.

4. Heat the remaining fat in a pan and fry the joint carefully to brown all over. Transfer to a casserole.

5. Stir the flour into the pan juices and cook for 1 minute. Gradually add the stock and Marsala and bring to the boil for 1 minute.

6. Add salt and pepper and the lemon juice and pour over the lamb. Cover the casserole and cook in a preheated oven for about 1½ hours or until tender.

7. Remove the lamb from the casserole and take off the string. Cut into thick slices and arrange on a hot plate. Garnish the sliced lamb with a few celery leaves and sprinkle with toasted nuts. Strain the sauce and serve in jug. If the sauce is too thick, add a little boiling stock.

LEFT TO RIGHT: Lamb lasagne; Fillets of lamb Marsala

Californian pork fillet

2 pork fillets, about 675 g (1½ lb)	3-4 tablespoons double cream (optional)
salt	sprigs of fresh herbs, to garnish
freshly ground black pepper	Stuffing:
2 tablespoons oil or dripping	50 g (2 oz) stoned prunes,
1 onion, peeled and chopped	soaked overnight and chopped
150 ml (¼ pint) beef stock	50 g (2 oz) fresh breadcrumbs
4 tablespoons white wine	1 small onion, peeled and finely
100 g (4 oz) stoned prunes,	chopped
soaked overnight	½ teaspoon dried thyme
2 tablespoons brandy (optional)	1 egg yolk

Preparation time: *20 minutes, plus overnight soaking*
Cooking time: *1 hour*
Oven: *180°C, 350°F, Gas Mark 4*

Stoned prunes which need no soaking are available, thus cutting out the necessity of remembering to soak the prunes in good time.

1. Split the pork fillets open a little with a sharp knife and sprinkle with salt and pepper.
2. To make the stuffing, mix the prunes, breadcrumbs, onion, thyme, salt and pepper, then bind together with the egg yolk. Spread over one piece of pork, cover with the second piece and secure with string.
3. Heat the oil or dripping in a pan and fry the piece of pork until browned all over. Transfer to a shallow ovenproof dish.
4. Fry the onion in the same fat until lightly browned. Drain off all the fat, then add the stock, wine, prunes and salt and pepper to the pan and bring to the boil.
5. Warm the brandy (if using), pour over the pork and ignite carefully. Pour the sauce over and around the pork and cover the dish with a lid or foil.
6. Cook in a preheated oven for about 1 hour until tender.
7. Remove the string from the pork and cut into slices. Add the cream to the sauce if preferred, adjust the seasoning and replace the pork in the sauce. Garnish with sprigs of fresh herbs.

Pork fillet Calvados

675 g (1½ lb) pork fillet, cut into 2 cm (¾ inch) slices	150 ml (¼ pint) chicken stock
salt	150 ml (¼ pint) single cream
freshly ground black pepper	2 teaspoons cornflour
40 g (1½ oz) butter or margarine	To garnish:
175 g (6 oz) mushrooms, sliced	40 g (1½ oz) hazelnuts, toasted and roughly chopped
3 tablespoons Calvados (or a miniature bottle)	1-2 teaspoons chopped fresh thyme
	1 tablespoon chopped fresh parsley

Preparation time: *10 minutes*
Cooking time: *45 minutes*
Oven: *180°C, 350°F, Gas Mark 4*

1. Sprinkle the pork slices lightly with salt and pepper. Melt 25 g (1 oz) of the fat in a frying pan, then fry the meat gently to seal. Transfer to a casserole.
2. Add the remaining fat and the mushrooms to the frying pan and cook gently for 2-3 minutes.
3. Add the Calvados, stock and salt and pepper to the pan and bring to the boil. Simmer uncovered for 2 minutes.
4. Pour the sauce over the pork and cover the casserole. Cook in a preheated oven for about 40 minutes or until tender.
5. Blend the cream with the cornflour, then stir into the sauce and return to the oven for 5-10 minutes until thickened.
6. Meanwhile mix the toasted hazelnuts with the chopped thyme and parsley. Sprinkle over the casserole and serve.

Variation:
Pork fillet is now easily obtainable from most butchers and larger supermarkets. It is a fairly expensive cut but is solid meat, with no fat and no waste at all. However if you can't find pork fillet, it can be substituted with boneless chicken breasts or thick fillets or breasts of turkey, or lamb fillet. The chicken should be either split in half if very thick or left as it is. Turkey breast can be cut into slanting slices of about 2 cm (¾ inch) thick. Cook in the same way as for pork.

Calvados is not always readily available in miniature bottles and it is expensive to buy a whole bottle if it is not one of your favourite drinks. Brandy can be used instead or try using 2 tablespoons of any orange liqueur and 1 tablespoon lemon juice; this combination will alter the flavour but make a tasty alternative.

LEFT TO RIGHT: Californian pork fillet; Pork fillet Calvados

Ragged rabbit

25 g (1 oz) butter or margarine	450 ml (¾ pint) chicken stock
1 tablespoon oil	4 carrots, peeled and diced
450 g (1 lb) boneless rabbit, diced	8-12 prunes, soaked (if necessary)
4 rashers bacon, derinded and chopped	salt
	freshly ground black pepper
350 g (12 oz) pickling onions, peeled	1 bay leaf
	4 tablespoons double cream (optional)
2 tablespoons flour	
150 ml (¼ pint) dry white wine	fresh bay leaves, to garnish

Preparation time: *25 minutes*
Cooking time: *1½ hours*
Oven: *180°C, 350°F, Gas Mark 4*

1. Heat the butter with the oil in a pan and fry the rabbit until browned. Transfer to a casserole.
2. Fry the bacon and onions in the same fat until lightly coloured. Sprinkle in the flour and cook for 1 minute.
3. Gradually add the wine and stock and bring to the boil for 2 minutes.
4. Add the carrots, prunes, salt and pepper and the bay leaf, then pour over the rabbit. Mix well and cover the casserole tightly.
5. Cook in a preheated oven for 1½ hours or until tender.
6. Taste and adjust the seasoning, discard the bay leaf and stir in the cream (if using). Serve garnished with fresh bay leaves.

Veal and Madeira casserole

25 g (1 oz) butter or margarine	2 tablespoons flour
1 tablespoon oil	450 ml (¾ pint) chicken stock
675 g (1½ lb) pie veal, cubed	4 tablespoons Madeira
175 g (6 oz) button onions, peeled	salt
	freshly ground black pepper
225 g (8 oz) carrots, peeled and diced	100 g (4 oz) mushrooms, sliced
	2 bay leaves
1 small red pepper, deseeded and sliced	

Preparation time: *20 minutes*
Cooking time: *1¼ - 1½ hours*
Oven: *180°C, 350°F, Gas Mark 4*

1. Heat the butter and oil in a pan and fry the veal until lightly browned. Transfer to a casserole.
2. Fry the onions and carrots for a few minutes in the same fat until beginning to brown, then add the pepper and continue cooking for about 2 minutes.
3. Stir in the flour and cook for 1 minute, then gradually add the stock and Madeira and bring to the boil. Add salt and pepper to taste, the mushrooms and bay leaves. Pour the mixture over the veal.

4. Cover the casserole tightly and cook in a preheated oven for 1¼ - 1½ hours until tender.
5. Discard the bay leaves, adjust the seasoning and serve with boiled rice.

Veal blanquette

90 g (3½ oz) butter	freshly ground black pepper
750 g (1¾ lb) leg of veal, boned and cubed	40 g (1½ oz) flour
	4 tablespoons double cream
2 small onions, peeled	2 tablespoons brandy
1 bouquet garni	To garnish:
300 ml (½ pint) white wine	fried button mushrooms
300 ml (½ pint) chicken stock	fried button onions
salt	watercress

Preparation time: *25 minutes*
Cooking time: *1¼ hours*
Oven: *160°C, 325°F, Gas Mark 3*

1. Melt 50 g (2 oz) of the butter in a pan and fry the veal until well sealed. Transfer to a casserole. Add the whole onions and bouquet garni. Bring the wine to the boil, season, and pour over the veal.
2. Cover and cook in a preheated oven for about 1 hour or until tender.
3. Discard the onions and bouquet garni. Strain off the cooking liquid and boil rapidly in a saucepan until reduced to 450 ml (¾ pint). Keep the veal warm.
4. Cream the remaining butter with the flour; gradually whisk into the sauce until thickened. Simmer for 3 minutes, adjust the seasoning and add cream.
5. Warm the brandy, pour over the veal and ignite carefully. Pour the sauce over the veal and garnish with the mushrooms, onions and watercress.

Paprika veal

25 g (1 oz) butter or margarine	1 tablespoon lemon juice
2 tablespoons oil	salt
675 g (1½ lb) pie veal, cubed	freshly ground black pepper
2 large onions, peeled and sliced	1 × 425 g (15 oz) can tomatoes
1 tablespoon paprika	50 g (2 oz) raisins
25 g (1 oz) flour	To garnish
300 ml (½ pint) chicken stock	5 cm (2 inch) piece cucumber
1 tablespoon tomato purée	4-6 tablespoons soured cream

Preparation time: *25 minutes*
Cooking time: *1¼ -1½ hours*
Oven: *180°C, 350°F, Gas Mark 4*

1. Melt the fat with 1 tablespoon of the oil in a pan and fry the veal until browned. Transfer to a casserole.
2. Add the rest of the oil to the pan and fry the onions until golden brown. Stir in the paprika and flour and cook for 1 minute. Pour over the veal.

3. Add the tomato purée, lemon juice, salt and pepper, tomatoes together with their liquid and the raisins, then simmer for 1 minute. Pour over the veal.
4. Cover the casserole tightly and cook in a preheated oven for 1¼ -1½ hours or until tender. Taste and adjust the seasoning.
5. Coarsely grate the cucumber, without peeling; or finely dice if preferred. Mix with the soured cream and spoon over the casserole. For an alternative presentation, spoon the soured cream over the casserole and sprinkle with the cucumber.

LEFT TO RIGHT: Veal blanquette; Paprika veal

Pot roast lemon veal

Serves 6

1.5 kg (3 lb) shoulder of veal, boned
salt
freshly ground black pepper
15 g (½ oz) butter
300 ml (½ pint) medium cider or chicken stock
juice of 1 small lemon
1 tablespoon cornflour

Stuffing
25 g (1 oz) butter
2 sticks celery, finely chopped
1 small onion, peeled and chopped
50 g (2 oz) mushrooms, chopped
1 small apple, peeled, cored and coarsely grated
50 g (2 oz) fresh white breadcrumbs
1 tablespoon chopped fresh parsley
1 tablespoon chopped fresh thyme or 1 teaspoon dried thyme
grated rind of 1 lemon
1 egg yolk

To garnish
175 g (6 oz) button mushrooms, fried
parsley sprigs
lemon wedges

Preparation time: *30 minutes*
Cooking time: *about 2 hours*
Oven: *180°C, 350°F, Gas Mark 4*

1. Lay the meat out flat and sprinkle with salt and pepper.

2. To make the stuffing, melt the butter in a pan and fry the celery and onion, until soft. Add the mushrooms and continue cooking for a few minutes.

3. Remove from the heat and mix with the apple, breadcrumbs, parsley, thyme, half the lemon rind, salt and pepper and bind together with the egg yolk.

4. Spread the stuffing over the meat and roll up carefully to enclose it. Secure with string.

5. Heat the butter in a pan and fry the joint until well browned all over. Transfer to a casserole or roasting tin.

6. Boil the cider or stock in a saucepan and pour with the lemon juice over the joint. Add salt and pepper and the remaining lemon rind and cover with a lid or foil.

7. Cook in a preheated oven for 1 hour. Baste and cook for further 1 hour. Transfer to a warm serving dish.

8. Blend the cornflour with a little cold water and add to the pan juices. Bring to the boil for 2 minutes, adjust the seasoning and serve in a jug.

9. Serve the veal cut into slices, garnished with fried mushrooms, parsley and lemon wedges.

CLOCKWISE FROM THE LEFT: Pot roast lemon veal; Party bacon; Veal and ham rolls

Party bacon

Serves 4-6

1.5 kg (3-3½ lb) gammon or prime collar bacon joint	75 g (3 oz) demerara sugar
	1 tablespoon dry mustard
1 × 425 g (15 oz) can peach halves	¼ teaspoon grated nutmeg
	watercress, to garnish
2 tablespoons wine vinegar	2-3 teaspoons cornflour
1 tablespoon lemon juice	(optional)
whole cloves	

Preparation time: *10 minutes, plus soaking*
Cooking time: *about 2¼ hours*
Oven: *190°C, 345°F, Gas Mark 5*

1. Soak the bacon in cold water; overnight if a smoked joint or 2-3 hours if unsmoked. Drain.
2. Place in a casserole large enough to hold the joint. Drain the peaches and pour the juice around the bacon. Add the vinegar, lemon juice and about 8 cloves.
3. Cover the casserole tightly and cook in a preheated oven for 1½ hours.
4. Remove the bacon from the casserole. Carefully strip the skin off the bacon and score the fat. Baste with the pan juices. Combine the sugar, mustard and nutmeg and sprinkle over the scored fat, then, if preferred, stud with cloves. Cook for a further 30 minutes.
5. Stud each peach half with 3 cloves and arrange around the joint; return to the oven for 10 minutes.
6. Serve on a hot dish surrounded by peach halves and garnished with watercress. The pan juices can be thickened with 2-3 teaspoons cornflour blended with a little cold water and brought to the boil; adjust the seasoning and serve with the joint.

Oxtail in beer

1 large oxtail, cut up	300 ml (½ pint) beef stock
seasoned flour	1 tablespoon tomato purée
2 tablespoons oil or dripping	salt
2 large onions, peeled and sliced	freshly ground black pepper
	1 tablespoon brown sugar
2 sticks celery, sliced	1 tablespoon vinegar
2 large carrots, peeled and sliced	2 bay leaves
	¼ teaspoon grated nutmeg
300 ml (½ pint) brown ale	

Preparation time: *15 minutes*
Cooking time: *3 hours, plus reheating*
Oven: *160°C, 325°F, Gas Mark 3*

1. Trim off any excess fat from the oxtail, then coat the pieces in seasoned flour.
2. Heat the oil or dripping in a pan and fry the oxtail until browned, then transfer to a large casserole with all the vegetables.

3. Heat the ale and stock in a saucepan, then add the tomato purée, salt, pepper, sugar, vinegar, bay leaves and nutmeg; bring to the boil and pour over the oxtail.
4. Cover the casserole tightly and cook in a preheated oven for about 3 hours or until tender. Cool, then chill.
5. Next day, remove fat, discard the bay leaves and return the casserole to a preheated oven for 1 hour before serving.

Veal and ham rolls

4 veal escalopes (about 100 g (4 oz) each) beaten	1 onion, peeled and sliced
	40 g (1½ oz) flour
4 slices cooked ham	250 ml (8 fl oz) chicken stock
salt	125 ml (4 fl oz) dry white wine
freshly ground black pepper	1 teaspoon mushroom ketchup
grated nutmeg	4 tablespoons single cream
1 × 225 g (8 oz) packet frozen leaf spinach, thawed	100 g (4 oz) mushrooms, quartered or sliced
25 g (1 oz) butter or margarine	parsley, to garnish
2 tablespoons oil	

Preparation time: *15 minutes*
Cooking time: *about 1 hour*
Oven: *180°C, 350°F, Gas Mark 4*

1. Lay the escalopes out on a flat surface. Cover each with a slice of ham and sprinkle with salt, pepper and nutmeg.
2. Squeeze out excess water from the spinach and divide into 4 equal portions. Place one on each escalope, roll up and secure with wooden cocktail sticks.
3. Heat the fat and oil in a pan and fry the veal until lightly browned. Remove to a casserole.
4. Fry the onion gently in the same fat, until soft. Stir in the flour, cook for 1 minute, then gradually add the stock and wine and bring to the boil.
5. Add the remaining ingredients and pour over veal. Cover and cook in a preheated oven for 1 hour.
6. Remove the cocktail sticks and serve garnished with parsley.

Medallions of veal with tarragon

8 medallions of veal, total weight about 1 kg (2 lb)	2 teaspoons lemon juice
salt	2 teaspoons dried tarragon or 4 teaspoons chopped fresh tarragon
freshly ground black pepper	
50 g (2 oz) butter	To garnish:
1 tablespoon finely chopped onion	100 g (4 oz) shortcrust pastry
	beaten egg, to glaze
2 tablespoons flour	sesame seeds
300 ml (½ pint) milk	fresh tarragon or parsley
150 ml (¼ pint) chicken stock	

Preparation time: *15 minutes*
Cooking time: *about 1 hour*
Oven: *180°C, 350°F, Gas Mark 4;*
200°C, 400°F, Gas Mark 6

Medallions of veal may be hard to find but you can also use small slices of fillet of veal, cut about 2 cm (¾ inch) thick.

1. Sprinkle the pieces of veal with salt and pepper.
2. Melt the butter in a pan and fry the pieces of veal to seal. Transfer to a shallow casserole.
3. Fry the onion gently in the fat remaining in the pan until soft. Stir in the flour and cook for 1 minute.
4. Graduually add the milk and stock and bring to the boil. Add the lemon juice, tarragon and salt and pepper, then pour over the veal.
5. Cover the casserole with a lid or foil and cook in a preheated oven for about 50 minutes or until tender.
6. To make pastry circles for the garnish, roll, out the shortcrust pastry and cut into 7 cm (2½ inch) fluted rounds. Place on a dampened baking sheet and prick well. Brush with egg and sprinkle with sesame seeds. Bake in a preheated oven at the higher temperature for 10-15 minutes until golden brown. Cool on a wire rack and reheat gently when required.
7. Garnish with pastry circles and fresh tarragon or parsley. Serve with duchesse potatoes and courgettes.

Variation:
This cut of veal can be expensive; an alternative is to use thick turkey fillets, cut into slanting slices about 2 cm (¾ inch) thick. Slices from a turkey breast joint, or boneless chicken breasts can also be used. Remove skin from chicken breasts and cut into slices or in half. The cooking time can be cut by about 15 minutes when using poultry. Try using fresh or dried sage instead of tarragon.

St Mellons rabbit

675 g (1½ lb) rabbit joints	2 teaspoons brown sugar
25 g (1 oz) seasoned flour	salt
175 g (6 oz) piece salt belly pork	freshly ground black pepper
2 tablespoons oil or dripping	2 carrots, peeled and sliced
2 onions, peeled and cut into wedges	2 slices bread, crusts removed
	1 egg, beaten
300 ml (½ pint) pale ale	2 tablespoons milk
150 ml (¼ pint) beef stock	100 g (4 oz) button mushrooms, trimmed and halved
1 tablespoon French mustard	
1 tablespoon wine vinegar	chopped fresh parsley, to garnish

Preparation time: *20 minutes*
Cooking time: *about 2 hours*
Oven: *180°C, 350°F, Gas Mark 4;*
        200°C, 400°F, Gas Mark 6

Some people feel rabbit has a strong flavour and prefer to soak it in cold water with 2 tablespoons vinegar or lemon juice added, for about 2 hours before rinsing, drying and cooking. If salt pork is unavailable use smoked bacon instead.

1. Cut the rabbit into smallish pieces if the joints are rather large, then coat in seasoned flour. Remove the skin from the pork and cut into dice, discarding any bones or gristle.
2. Heat the oil in a pan and fry the pieces of rabbit and pork until well browned. Transfer to a casserole.
3. Fry the onions in the same fat until lightly browned, then sprinkle on the remaining seasoned flour. Gradually add the ale and stock and bring to the boil.
4. Stir in the mustard, vinegar, sugar and salt and pepper, then add the carrots. Pour over the rabbit.
5. Cover the casserole and cook in a preheated oven for 1½ hours.
6. Cut the bread into squares or triangles. Whisk the egg and milk together with salt and pepper and dip the bread into it. Increase the oven temperature.
7. Remove the lid from the casserole, give a gentle stir and taste and adjust the seasoning. Add the mushrooms. Lay the egg-soaked bread on top of the casserole and return to the oven, uncovered, for 20-30 minutes or until crisp and lightly browned. Serve sprinkled with chopped parsley.

CLOCKWISE FROM THE BOTTOM: Herries pork; St Mellons rabbit; Tipsy pork and potatoes

If using frozen rabbit make sure it is completely thawed before cooking. The casserole may be frozen for up to 2 months; it makes no difference if the dish is made with frozen or fresh rabbit, it can be frozen a second time once it has been cooked, although refreezing may affect the eating quality and texture. The casserole can also be made into a traditional puff-topped rabbit pie. Turn into a deep pie dish with a funnel in the centre. Cover with a lid made using about 225 g (8 oz) puff pastry after putting a 2.5 cm (1 inch) strip around the rim of the dish. Flute and crimp the edge, glaze the top with beaten egg and decorate with pastry leaves. Glaze again and make a hole in the centre. Cook in a hot oven (220°C, 425°F, Gas Mark 7) for 20 minutes, then reduce to moderately hot (190°C, 375°F, Gas Mark 5) and continue for 25-30 minutes or until puffed up and golden brown.

1. Melt 25 g (1 oz) of the butter in a pan and fry the pork cubes until browned. Transfer to a casserole.
2. Melt the remaining butter in the pan and add the onion, celery, pepper and garlic. Cook over a high heat for 2 minutes, stirring frequently, then transfer to the casserole.
3. Combine the sherry, soy sauce and lemon juice and make up to 300 ml (½ pint) with stock. Add salt and pepper, then the water chestnuts. Stir into the onion mixture.
4. Pour the sauce over the pork, mix well and cover.
5. Cook in a preheated oven for 50-60 minutes or until tender. Taste and adjust the seasoning.
6. Meanwhile melt the butter for the topping in a frying pan and fry the breadcrumbs until beginning to brown. Add the nuts and continue frying until golden brown.
7. Serve the casserole with the nut topping spooned over and garnished with parsley.

Tipsy pork and potatoes

1 tablespoon oil	6 gherkins, sliced
4-6 boneless pork chops, about 450 g (1 lb), cut into 1 cm (½ inch) strips	salt
	freshly ground black pepper
	6 tablespoons dry white wine
1 kg (2 lb) potatoes, peeled and thinly sliced	150 ml (¼ pint) single cream
	chopped fresh continental parsley, to garnish
2 medium onions, peeled and thinly sliced	

Preparation time: *15 minutes*
Cooking time: *about 2¼ hours*
Oven: *180°C, 350°F, Gas Mark 4;*
200°C, 400°F, Gas Mark 6

1. Heat the oil in a frying pan and fry the meat quickly, just to seal.
2. Layer the potatoes in a lightly greased heavy ovenproof casserole with the pieces of pork, onions, gherkins and season with salt and pepper.
3. Mix the wine and cream together well and pour over the potatoes.
4. Cover the casserole and cook in a preheated oven for 1¼ hours. Remove the casserole and increase the oven temperature.
5. Remove the lid and return to the oven for 30-40 minutes until the potatoes are golden brown and crisp on top. Serve with parsley.

Herries pork

50 g (2 oz) butter or margarine	salt
675 g (1½ lb) lean pork, cut into 2.5 cm (1 inch) cubes	freshly ground black pepper
	1 × 225 g (8 oz) can water chestnuts, drained, and sliced if large
1 onion, peeled and finely chopped	
4 sticks celery, thinly sliced	Topping:
1 large red pepper, deseeded and thinly sliced	40 g (1½ oz) butter
	40 g (1½ oz) fresh breadcrumbs
1-2 garlic cloves, peeled and crushed	40 g (1½ oz) blanched almonds, chopped
4 tablespoons medium sherry	chopped fresh parsley, to garnish
2 tablespoons soy sauce	
1 tablespoon lemon juice	
about 175 ml (6 fl oz) beef stock	

Preparation time: *15 minutes*
Cooking time: *about 1 hour*
Oven: *180°C, 350°F, Gas Mark 4*

Madeira bacon

Serves 4-6

1.5 kg (3 lb) prime collar bacon joint
150 ml (¼ pint) chicken stock
150 ml (¼ pint) Madeira
freshly ground black pepper
whole cloves
1 tablespoon oil or dripping
350 g (12 oz) pickling onions, peeled

350 g (12 oz) carrots, peeled and sliced
2-3 tablespoons fresh breadcrumbs
1 tablespoon cornflour
1 × 225 g (8 oz) packet frozen leaf spinach, cooked

Preparation time: *10 minutes, plus soaking*
Cooking time: *2-2¼ hours*
Oven: *190°C, 375°F, Gas Mark 5*

1. Soak the bacon in cold water; overnight if a smoked joint or 2-3 hours if unsmoked. Drain well and place in a casserole.
2. Bring the stock and Madeira to the boil, add plenty of pepper and pour over the bacon joint. Cover and cook in a preheated oven for 1 hour.
3. Remove the joint and strip off the skin. Stud the fat with cloves and return to the casserole, basting well.
4. Melt the oil or dripping in a pan and fry the onions until golden brown and arrange round the joint with the carrots. Cover and return to the oven for 45 minutes.
5. Remove the lid from the casserole, baste the bacon again and sprinkle the fat with breadcrumbs. Return to the oven, uncovered, for 15-20 minutes or until the joint is tender and the topping crisped and lightly browned.
6. Drain off the juices into a saucepan and thicken with the cornflour, blended in a little cold water. Bring back to the boil and adjust the seasoning.
7. Serve the joint on a warmed dish surrounded by the onions and carrots and small piles of cooked spinach. Put the sauce into a jug to serve separately.

Pot roast pork with aubergine

Serves 6

1.5 kg (3 lb) leg of pork, boned and rolled
salt
freshly ground black pepper
2 tablespoons oil
3 onions, peeled and cut into wedges
300 ml (½ pint) beef stock
1 tablespoon Worcestershire sauce

½ teaspoon ground coriander
1 large aubergine, trimmed, halved lengthways and sliced
2 large carrots, peeled and sliced
To garnish:
baked tomatoes
continental parsley

Preparation time: *15 minutes*
Cooking time: *about 2¼ hours*
Oven: *190°C, 375°F, Gas Mark 5*

1. Sprinkle the pork with salt and pepper. Heat the oil in a frying pan and fry the pork all over until browned. Transfer to a casserole.
2. Fry the onions in the same fat for 1 minute, then arrange round the pork.
3. Combine the stock and Worcestershire sauce, add salt and pepper and the coriander. Pour over the joint and cover the casserole.
4. Cook in a preheated oven for 1 hour.
5. Baste the joint, add the aubergine and carrots to the casserole, cover and return to the oven for a further 1-1¼ hours or until tender.
6. Remove the meat to a serving dish and arrange the drained vegetables around it.
7. Remove any fat from the surface of the pan juices, taste and adjust the seasoning and pour into a jug to serve with the pork. Garnish the joint with baked tomatoes and continental parsley if available. Otherwise use English parsley.

Smoked joints can also be used but are more likely to be salty than unsmoked (green) bacon and therefore need longer soaking in cold water. Allow up to 24 hours for smoked or 6 hours if green. Rinse thoroughly and, if boiling the joint, always cook in fresh water; 2 tablespoons sugar helps counteract the salt. When serving cold, leave the joint to cool in the cooking liquor, then strip off the skin. A cold bacon joint can be served with the fat simply sprinkled with dry breadcrumbs or with a glaze, such as brown sugar and mustard, spread over the scored fat, which is then 'set' by placing under a moderate grill for a few minutes.

To make the skin really crisp, stand in the casserole with skin upwards. After the initial cooking, add the vegetables to the casserole and cover just the vegetables with foil, moulding to the joint so that the vegetables will not dry out. Then brush the scored rind of the pork with oil and sprinkle with salt before returning to the oven.

Other cuts of pork, such as loin or hand, may also be used. Loin is a lot fattier, so it will need a good amount of fat skimmed from the surface of the pan juices before serving. Hand of pork is an economical cut and is a good joint for this recipe once it has been boned and rolled.

Pork Niçoise

40 g (1½ oz) butter or margarine
675 g (1½ lb) lean pork, cut into 2.5 cm (1 inch) cubes
2 onions, peeled and roughly chopped
1 garlic clove, peeled and crushed
1 tablespoon flour
150 ml (¼ pint) red wine
150 ml (¼ pint) beef stock

1 × 225 g (8 oz) can tomatoes
1 tablespoon tomato purée
salt
freshly ground black pepper
6 large gherkins, sliced
16 black olives
1 green pepper, deseeded, sliced and blanched
To garnish:
hard-boiled egg slices
anchovy fillets
parsley sprigs

Preparation time: *15 minutes*
Cooking time: *1½ hours*
Oven: *180°C, 350°F, Gas Mark 4*

1. Melt the fat in a frying pan and fry the meat until lightly browned. Transfer to a casserole.

2. Fry the onions and garlic in the same fat until soft. Stir in the flour and cook for 1 minute.
3. Gradually add the wine and stock and bring to the boil. Liquidize or purée the tomatoes and add to the sauce with the tomato purée, salt, pepper, gherkins and olives.
4. Pour over the casserole and cover tightly. Cook in a preheated oven for 1 hour.
5. Add the sliced pepper to the casserole, adjust the seasoning and return to the oven for 20-30 minutes or until tender, adding a little extra stock if the contents seem dry.
6. Serve garnished with slices of hard-boiled egg, anchovies and parsley.

LEFT TO RIGHT: Pork Niçoise; Pot roast pork with aubergine

POULTRY AND GAME

Chicken Marengo

1.75 kg (4 lb) chicken	150 ml (¼ pint) dry white wine
salt	1 tablespoon tomato purée
freshly ground black pepper	100 g (4 oz) button mushrooms,
50 g (2 oz) butter	trimmed and halved
2 tablespoons brandy	To garnish:
1 onion, peeled and sliced	4 crayfish or 8 large whole
1-2 garlic cloves, crushed	prawns
2 tablespoons flour	25 g (1 oz) butter
1 × 425 g (15 oz) can	2 hard-boiled eggs, quartered
tomatoes, liquidized, puréed or	few slices pickled walnut or 8
very finely chopped	black olives

Preparation time: *20 minutes*
Cooking time: *about 50 minutes*
Oven: *180°C, 350°F, Gas Mark 4*

1. Cut the chicken into 8 even-sized pieces and remove the skin. Sprinkle with salt and pepper.
2. Melt 25 g (1 oz) of the butter in a pan and fry the pieces of chicken until browned. Transfer to a casserole.
3. Warm the brandy, pour over the pieces of chicken and ignite carefully.
4. Add the remaining butter to the pan and then add the onion and garlic. Fry gently until lightly coloured.
5. Add the flour to the onions and cook for 1 minute. Gradually add the tomatoes, wine and tomato purée and bring to the boil.
6. Add salt and pepper and the mushrooms and simmer for 2 minutes. Pour over the chicken and cover the casserole.
7. Cook in a preheated oven for 45-50 minutes or until tender.
8. For the garnish, lightly fry the crayfish or prawns in butter. Arrange the chicken pieces on a deep serving plate, spoon the sauce over and garnish with crayfish or prawns, quarters of hard-boiled egg and slices of pickled walnut or black olives

Artichoke chicken

4 boneless chicken breasts	150 ml (¼ pint) dry white wine
salt	150 ml (¼ pint) chicken stock
freshly ground black pepper	6 tablespoons single cream
40 g (1¼ oz) butter or	1 × 425 g (15 oz) can artichoke
margarine	hearts, drained
1 onion, peeled and sliced	watercress, to garnish
2 tablespoons flour	

Preparation time: *10 minutes*
Cooking time: *about 1 hour*
Oven: *180°C, 350°F, Gas Mark 4*

Chicken portions or pieces of boneless chicken thigh meat may be used as well as boned breasts for this recipe.

1. Trim the chicken, remove the skin if liked, and sprinkle lightly with salt and pepper. Heat the fat in a pan and fry the chicken until browned all over. Transfer to a casserole.
2. Fry the onion gently in the same fat until soft but only lightly coloured.
3. Stir in the flour and cook for 1 minute. Gradually add the wine and stock and bring to the boil. Add the cream and plenty of salt and pepper and bring just back to the boil.
4. Cut each artichoke heart in half. Add to the pan, then pour the wine mixture over the chicken and cover the casserole.
5. Cook in a preheated oven for 50-60 minutes or until the chicken is very tender. Garnish with watercress.

Variation:
This makes a good filling for a pie too. Leave to become cold, then remove the pieces of chicken, chop roughly and return to the sauce. For a double crust pie allow approximately 350 g (12 oz) shortcrust pastry (made using 350 g (12 oz) plain flour). Roll out two-thirds to line a 23 cm (9 inch) deep pie plate or tin, cover with the remainder and brush with beaten eggs to glaze. Cook for about 45 minutes at 200°C, 400°F, Gas Mark 6.

TOP TO BOTTOM: Chicken Marengo; Artichoke chicken

Chicken Rossini

4 boneless chicken breasts	6 tablespoons chicken stock
salt	3 tablespoons double cream
freshly ground black pepper	(optional)
about 100 g (4 oz) firm pâté	To garnish:
40 g (1½ oz) butter	4 slices bread
175 g (6 oz) button mushrooms,	25 g (1 oz) butter
sliced	2 tablespoons oil
3 tablespoons brandy	watercress

Preparation time: *15 minutes*
Cooking time: *about 40 minutes*
Oven: *180°C, 350°F, Gas Mark 4*

1. Remove the skin from the pieces of chicken and flatten a little. Sprinkle lightly with salt and pepper.
2. Cut the pâté into 4 even slices and wrap up in pieces of chicken. Secure with fine string or wooden cocktail sticks.
3. Melt the butter in a pan and fry the chicken until lightly browned. Transfer to a casserole.
4. Fry the mushrooms gently in the same fat for about 1 minute, then add the brandy and stock and bring to the boil. Add salt and pepper and pour the mixture over the chicken.
5. Cover the casserole and cook in a preheated oven for about 40 minutes or until cooked through.
6. Cut the bread into ovals about the size of the chicken pieces and fry in a mixture of butter and oil until golden.
7. Place the bread croûtons on a hot serving dish and top each with a portion of chicken (after removing the string or cocktail sticks). Adjust the seasoning in the sauce, add cream (if using) and reheat. Spoon over and around the chicken. Garnish with watercress.

Chicken Rossini

Guinea fowl Normandy

Serves 6

2 plump guinea fowl	3 tablespoons brandy or
salt	Calvados (optional)
freshly ground black pepper	300 ml (½ pint) single cream
1 small orange, quartered	To garnish:
75 g (3 oz) butter	watercress
675 g (1½ lb) cooking apples, peeled, cored and sliced	spring onions
grated rind of ½ orange or lemon	

Preparation time: *15-20 minutes*
Cooking time: *1¾-1½ hours*
Oven: *180°C, 350°F, Gas Mark 4*

1. Sprinkle the guinea fowl lightly with salt and pepper and put 2 quarters of orange in the cavity of each bird.
2. Melt 25 g (1 oz) butter in a pan and fry the birds until browned all over. Remove from the pan.
3. Arrange half the apples in a large deep casserole or roasting tin. Sprinkle with orange or lemon rind and salt and pepper. Stand the guinea fowl on top and arrange the rest of the apples round them.
4. Melt the remaining butter and pour over the guinea fowl, then pour over the brandy or Calvados (if using).
5. Cover the casserole with a lid or foil and cook in a preheated oven for 1½-1¾ hours or until quite tender. Fifteen minutes before the end of the cooking, uncover, to brown the birds, and spoon over the single cream.
6. Either serve from the casserole or spoon the apple mixture on to a large serving platter and put the guinea fowl in the centre. Garnish with watercress and onions.

Baked hare with cream sauce

Serves 4-6

1 young hare, prepared and jointed	150 ml (¼ pint) beef stock
300 ml (½ pint) dry white wine	6 tablespoons double cream
4 tablespoons oil	2 teaspoons cornflour
3-4 fresh bay leaves	To garnish:
salt	cubes of fried bread
freshly ground black pepper	bacon rolls
	fresh bay leaves

Preparation time: *15 minutes, plus marinating*
Cooking time: *about 2 hours*
Oven: *180°C, 350°F, Gas Mark 4*

1. Place hare in a large flameproof casserole with the wine, oil, bay leaves, salt and plenty of black pepper. Cover and marinate for at least 4 hours and up to 36 hours. Turn the hare several times.
2. Add the stock, cover the casserole and cook in a preheated oven for 2 hours, stirring after 1 hour.

3. Remove the hare to a hot serving dish and keep warm. Discard the bay leaves and skim off any surplus fat.
4. Blend the cream with the cornflour and stir into the cooking juices. Reheat, bringing back to the boil for 1 minute and adjust the seasoning.
5. Pour the sauce back over the hare and garnish with bread, bacon rolls and bay leaves.

Pigeons Louisette

1 small orange, quartered	1 tablespoon flour
4 plump pigeons	6-8 tablespoons Marsala or
salt	sherry
freshly ground black pepper	300 ml (½ pint) chicken stock
8 rashers streaky bacon, derinded	100 g (4 oz) button mushrooms, quartered
25 g (1 oz) butter or margarine	6 juniper berries, crushed
1 tablespoon oil	3-4 tablespoons cream (optional)
1 large onion, peeled and chopped	parsley, to garnish

Preparation time: *20-25 minutes*
Cooking time: *about 1½ hours*
Oven: *180°C, 350°F, Gas Mark 4*

1. Place a piece of orange inside the cavity of each pigeon. Sprinkle lightly with salt and pepper and lay 2 bacon rashers over each bird. Secure with string.
2. Heat the fat and oil in a pan and fry the pigeons until browned all over. Transfer to a casserole.
3. Fry the onion in the same fat until lightly browned. Stir in the flour and cook for 1 minute. Gradually add the Marsala and stock and bring to the boil.
4. Add the mushrooms, juniper berries and season with salt and pepper. Pour over the pigeons.
5. Cover the casserole and cook in a preheated oven for 1-1½ hours or until very tender.
6. Remove the string from the pigeons. Skim, then spoon off a little of the juices, blend with the cream and stir back into the sauce. Serve garnished with parsley.

Poacher's casserole

Serves 4-6

1 pheasant, quartered	4 carrots, peeled and sliced
1 grouse, halved or quartered	2 tablespoons flour
2 pigeons, halved	1 tablespoon capers
salt	300 ml (½ pint) dry cider
freshly ground black pepper	300 ml (½ pint) beef stock
2 tablespoons oil	2 bay leaves
175 g (6 oz) piece streaky bacon, derinded and chopped	chopped fresh parsley, to garnish
2 large onions, peeled and sliced	

Preparation time: *20 minutes*
Cooking time: *about 1½ hours*
Oven: *160°C, 325°F, Gas Mark 3*

Game is easier to find now that it is available frozen from supermarkets. Any game can be used for this casserole or just one type mixed with pieces of chicken to make it a more economical but tasty dish.

1. Wipe the pieces of game and sprinkle with salt and pepper. Heat the oil in a pan and fry the game with bacon until browned all over. Transfer to a casserole.
2. Fry the onions and carrots in the same fat until lightly browned, stir in the flour, then add the capers, cider, stock, salt and pepper and the bay leaves. Bring to the boil.
3. Pour over the game, cover the casserole tightly and cook in a preheated oven for about 1½ hours or until tender.
4. Discard the bay leaves, adjust the seasoning and skim any fat from the surface of the casserole. Sprinkle thickly with chopped parsley and serve with creamy mashed potatoes.

Wild duck and some grouse are in season from 12th August to 10th December; but pheasants and partridges continue until February. Game shot in season can be sold frozen for a while after the end of the season but only a few specialized shops will sell them; it is best to buy fresh whilst in season and freeze for your own use. Any type of game can be used for the Poacher's casserole, either a single variety or any combination which is available. Partridges should be halved, wild duck halved if small, or quartered if a larger duck, such as mallard, or use venison cut into 4 cm (1½ inch) cubes.

Pigeon and steak casserole

2 pigeons, halved	150 ml (¼ pint) red wine
350 g (12 oz) braising steak, cut into 2.5 cm (1 inch) cubes	100 g (4 oz) button mushrooms, trimmed and halved
salt	1 bay leaf
freshly ground black pepper	2-3 tomatoes, peeled and quartered (optional)
25 g (1 oz) butter or margarine	Caraway balls:
1 tablespoon oil	100 g (4 oz) fresh breadcrumbs
100 g (4 oz) piece back bacon, derinded and diced	25 g (1 oz) shredded suet
225 g (8 oz) pickling onions, peeled	¼-½ teaspoon caraway seeds a little beaten egg
1 tablespoon flour	fat for frying
450 ml (¾ pint) beef stock	

Preparation time: *about 20 minutes*
Cooking time: *about 1¾ hours*
Oven: *180°C, 350°F, Gas Mark 4*

1. Wipe the pieces of pigeon. Sprinkle the pigeon and steak with salt and pepper.
2. Heat the fat and oil in a pan and fry the pigeons and steak until well sealed. Transfer to a casserole.
3. Fry the bacon and onions in the same fat until lightly browned. Add the flour and cook for 1 minute.
4. Gradually add the stock and wine and bring to the boil. Add the mushrooms, bay leaf and tomatoes and pour into the casserole.
5. Cover the casserole tightly and cook in a preheated oven for about 1¾ hours or until tender.
6. To make the caraway balls, combine the breadcrumbs, suet, caraway seeds and salt and pepper. Bind together with beaten egg. Divide and shape into 4 balls. Melt fat in a pan and fry for about 5 minutes, until golden brown.
7. Discard the bay leaf from the casserole and serve with the caraway balls on top.

Variation:
Replace the pigeons with a hen pheasant cut into quarters and use white wine or cider in place of red wine.

Christmas venison roast

Serves 6-8

2.25 kg (5 lb) haunch of venison	450 ml (¾ pint) stock (see method)
1 onion, peeled and sliced	
1 carrot, peeled and sliced	5-6 tablespoons port
2 bay leaves	3 tablespoons cranberry jelly
175 g (6 oz) streaky bacon rashers, derinded	2 teaspoons lemon juice
salt	225 g (8 oz) small button mushrooms, trimmed
freshly ground black pepper	To garnish:
1 tablespoon dripping or oil	canned artichokes
1 tablespoon flour	watercress

Preparation time: *15 minutes*
Cooking time: *about 2½ hours*
Oven: *160°C, 325°F, Gas Mark 3*

1. Bone the venison and use the bones to make stock, using 1.2 litres (2 pints) water, the onion, carrot and bay leaves. Simmer for about 1 hour.
2. The boned venison should weigh about 1.75 kg (4 lb). Roll up neatly, arrange the bacon rashers evenly over the joint and secure with string. Sprinkle with salt and pepper.

3. Heat the dripping or oil in a pan and fry the venison until browned all over. Transfer to a deep casserole.
4. Stir the flour into the fat and juices left in the pan and cook for 1 minute. Gradually add 450 ml (¾ pint) of the stock, the port, cranberry jelly and lemon juice and bring to the boil. Add salt and pepper and pour the mixture over the venison.
5. Cover the casserole tightly and cook in a preheated oven for about 2 hours. Add the mushrooms and continue for about 30 minutes or until very tender, basting several times.
6. Remove the venison to a warmed serving dish and take off the string. Spoon off any fat from the sauce in the casserole, adjust the seasoning and serve in a sauceboat. Garnish the joint with canned artichokes and watercress.

LEFT TO RIGHT: Pigeon and steak casserole; Christmas venison roast

Jugged pheasant

1 cock pheasant, cut into quarters or eighths	salt
	freshly ground black pepper
Marinade:	**Stuffing balls:**
1 onion, peeled and sliced	25 g (1 oz) butter or margarine
2 tablespoons oil	1 small onion, peeled and grated
6 peppercorns	
1 tablespoon lemon juice	2 sticks celery, very finely chopped
150 ml (¼ pint) red wine	
Casserole:	grated rind of ½ lemon
2 tablespoons dripping or oil	pinch of grated nutmeg
2 onions, peeled and chopped	100 g (4 oz) fresh breadcrumbs
2 sticks celery, sliced	1 tablespoon chopped fresh parsley
2 carrots, peeled and sliced	
1½-2 tablespoons flour	1 egg yolk
300 ml (½ pint) water	**To garnish:**
1 meat stock cube	grilled bacon rolls
1 tablespoon redcurrant jelly	parsley
2 bay leaves	

Preparation time: *25-30 minutes, plus marinating*
Cooking time: *1½ hours*
Oven: *160°C, 325°F, Gas Mark 3*

1. Place the pieces of pheasant in a bowl. Add the marinade ingredients and marinate for 3 hours
2. Drain the pheasant, strain the marinade and discard the onion and peppercorns. Heat the fat in a pan and fry the pheasant until brown. Transfer to a casserole.
3. Add the vegetables to the pan and fry gently until golden brown, stirring from time to time. Sprinkle on the flour and cook for 1 minute, then gradually add the marinade, water, stock cube, redcurrant jelly, bay leaves and seasoning. Pour over the pheasant.
4. Cover the casserole tightly and cook in a preheated oven for 1½ hours or until tender.
5. To make the stuffing balls, melt the fat in a pan and fry the onion and celery gently until soft. Add all the other ingredients, binding together with the egg yolk.
6. Shape the mixture into balls. Place in a greased ovenproof dish and cook for 30 minutes.
7. Skim off any excess fat. Add the stuffing balls to the casserole and garnish with bacon rolls and parsley.

Turkey beanpot

25 g (1 oz) butter or margarine
1 tablespoon oil
675 g (1½ lb) raw turkey thigh meat, skinned and cut into 2.5 cm (1 inch) cubes
1 large onion, peeled and sliced
1 garlic clove, peeled and crushed
1 red pepper, deseeded and chopped
1 tablespoon flour
150 ml (¼ pint) red wine

1 × 425 g (15 oz) can tomatoes
150 ml (¼ pint) chicken stock
salt
freshly ground black pepper
1 teaspoon ground ginger
1 tablespoon soy sauce
1 tablespoon Worcestershire sauce
1 × 200 g (7 oz) can butter beans, drained
1 × 425 g (15 oz) can red kidney beans, drained

Preparation time: *15 minutes*
Cooking time: *about 1 hour*
Oven: *180°C, 350°F, Gas Mark 4*

1. Heat the fat and oil in a pan and fry the turkey until lightly browned. Transfer to a casserole.
2. Fry the onion and garlic in the same fat until soft. Add the pepper and continue cooking for 2 minutes.
3. Stir in the flour and cook for 1 minute, then add the wine, tomatoes and stock and bring to the boil.
4. Add the remaining ingredients. Cover and cook in a preheated oven for 1 hour.

Plum duck

2.25-2.75 kg (5-6 lb) duck
salt
freshly ground black pepper
1 garlic clove, peeled and crushed
1 × 550 g (1¼ lb) can red plums in syrup

2 teaspoons Worcestershire sauce
1 tablespoon wine vinegar
watercress, to garnish

Preparation time: *10 minutes*
Cooking time: *about 1½ hours*
Oven: *200°C, 400°F, Gas Mark 6*

1. Remove any excess fat from the duck and place in a large casserole or roasting tin. Prick the skin all over with a fork, then sprinkle with salt, pepper and garlic.
2. Cook in a preheated oven for 30 minutes.
3. Spoon off all the fat from the pan, leaving just the pan juices around the duck.
4. Drain the juice from the plums, add the Worcestershire sauce, vinegar and salt and pepper and make up to 300 ml (½ pint) with water. Pour over the duck, cover with foil and return to the oven for 45 minutes.
5. Baste the duck with the juices again and arrange the plums around the bird. Cover and return to the oven for 15 minutes or until tender. The cover may be left off for the last 10 minutes to crisp up the skin.
6. Transfer the duck to a serving dish with the plums around and garnish with watercress. Spoon the fat off the pan juices, adjust the seasoning and serve in a sauce boat.

Duck with orange sauce

4 duck portions, about 300-425 g (11-15 oz) each, trimmed and excess fat removed	1 meat stock cube
	150 ml (¼ pint) boiling water
	juice of ½ lemon
salt	4 tablespoons port
freshly ground black pepper	2 tablespoons redcurrant or bramble jelly
2 oranges	To garnish:
1 tablespoon oil or dripping	orange segments
1 tablespoon flour	watercress

Preparation time: *25-30 minutes*
Cooking time: *50-60 minutes*
Oven: *180°C, 350°F, Gas Mark 4*

A whole duck can be cut into 4 portions as shown in the illustrations.

1. Prick the skin of the duck portions all over with a fork.

Sprinkle lightly with salt and pepper.
2. Pare the rind thinly from the oranges and cut into julienne strips; alternatively, grate the rind coarsely from the fruit. Squeeze out the juice.
3. Heat the oil or dripping in a pan and fry the duck until browned all over. Transfer the duck to a casserole. Pour off all but 1 tablespoon of the fat from the pan.
4. Stir the flour into the residue in the pan and cook for 1 minute. Dissolve the stock cube in the water and add to the pan with the orange juice, rind, lemon juice, port and redcurrant jelly.
5. Bring to the boil and simmer until the jelly has dissolved, then add salt and pepper and pour over the duck. Cover the casserole tightly. Cook in a preheated oven for 50-60 minutes or until the duck is tender.
6. Arrange the duck portions in a deep serving dish, spoon the sauce over and garnish with orange segments and watercress.

LEFT TO RIGHT: Plum duck; Duck with orange sauce

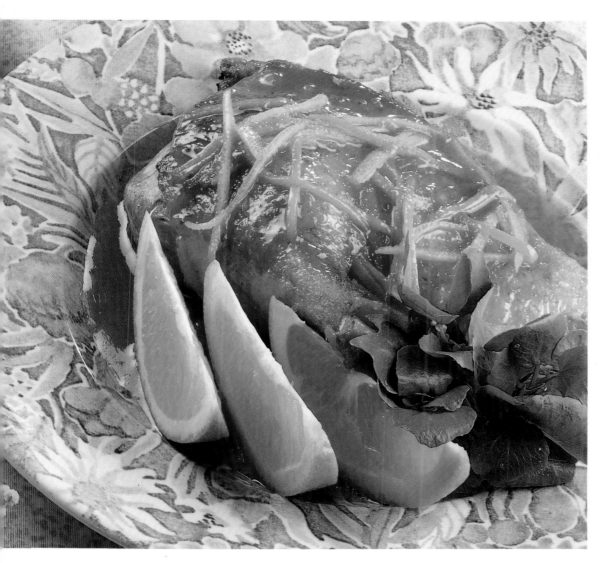

Cut in two breast side up.

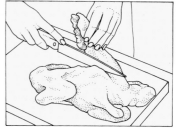

Cut out backbone and remove.

Cut each half in two.

Turkey Cinzano

4 thick turkey escalopes or breast fillets	1 tablespoon tomato purée
salt	125 ml (4 fl oz) Cinzano Bianco
freshly ground black pepper	2 teaspoons lemon juice
1 garlic clove, peeled and crushed	2 bay leaves
	To garnish:
25 g (1 oz) butter or margarine	fresh bay leaves or sprigs of parsley
1 × 425 g (15 oz) can tomatoes	lemon slices

Preparation time: *15 minutes*
Cooking time: *45-50 minutes*
Oven: *180°C, 350°F, Gas Mark 4*

1. Sprinkle the turkey escalopes with salt, pepper and garlic powder.
2. Melt the butter in a pan and fry the escalopes until lightly browned. Transfer to a shallow ovenproof casserole.

3. Liquidize or purée the canned tomatoes and add to the residue in the pan with the tomato purée. Cook until reduced by almost half and thickened.
4. Add the Cinzano and lemon juice to the pan, bring to the boil and add the salt, pepper and crushed garlic. Pour over the turkey, add the bay leaves and cover with foil or a lid.
5. Cook in a preheated oven for 45-50 minutes or until tender.
6. Adjust the seasoning, discard the bay leaves and serve garnished with bay leaves or parsley, and slices of lemon.

CLOCKWISE FROM THE BOTTOM: Chicken Véronique; Turkey Cinzano; Turkey fricassée

Turkey fricassée

675 g (1½ lb) boneless turkey breast, cut into 2.5 cm (1 inch) cubes	50 g (2 oz) butter or margarine
	100 g (4 oz) button mushrooms, trimmed and sliced
2 onions, peeled and chopped	40 g (1½ oz) flour
3 carrots, peeled and sliced	1 egg yolk
1 bay leaf	3 tablespoons double cream
about 450 ml (¾ pint) chicken stock	juice of ½ small lemon
salt	To garnish:
	bacon rolls
freshly ground black pepper	watercress

Preparation time: *20 minutes*
Cooking time: *1¼ hours*
Oven: *180°C, 350°F, Gas Mark 4*

1. Place the turkey in a casserole with the onions, carrots, and bay leaf.
2. Bring the stock to the boil, add plenty of salt and pepper and pour over the turkey just to cover. Cover the casserole.
3. Cook in a preheated oven for about 1 hour or until tender. Discard the bay leaf.
4. Strain off the juices from the turkey and reserve 450 ml (¾ pint); keep the turkey covered and warm.
5. Melt the butter in a pan and fry the mushrooms for 1 minute. Stir in the flour and cook for 1 minute, then gradually add the reserved stock and bring to the boil until thickened,. stirring frequently. Simmer for 2 minutes.
6. Blend the egg yolk with the cream, add a little of the sauce, then stir it all back into the sauce and reheat without boiling. Adjust the seasoning and stir in the lemon juice to sharpen the sauce.
7. Pour the sauce over the turkey, mix well and serve garnished with grilled bacon rolls and watercress.

Variation:
This recipe can be made equally well with veal or pork — use pie veal cut into cubes or any lean cut of pork, trimmed free of fat and skin, and cut into cubes. Cook as in the recipe but increase the initial cooking time to about 1½ hours or until the meat is tender. Replace 150 ml (¼ pint) of the stock with white wine or cider. 1-2 teaspoons freshly chopped tarragon or thyme may be added to the sauce if a herb flavoured casserole is preferred.

Chicken Véronique

4 chicken breasts, partly boned	grated rind of ½ lemon
salt	1 tablespoon lemon juice
freshly ground black pepper	1 bay leaf
25 g (1 oz) butter	150 ml (¼ pint) single cream
1 tablespoon oil	1 egg yolk
25 g (1 oz) flour	100 g (4 oz) green grapes, peeled, halved and seeded
150 ml (¼ pint) medium white wine	To garnish:
150 ml (¼ pint) chicken stock	green grapes or kiwi fruit
	watercress

Preparation time: *15 minutes*
Cooking time: *55-60 minutes*
Oven: *180°C, 350°F, Gas Mark 4*

1. Remove the skin from the chicken if liked, then sprinkle the pieces of chicken lightly with salt and pepper.
2. Heat the butter and oil in a pan and fry the chicken until lightly browned all over. Transfer to a casserole.
3. Stir the flour into the pan juices, then add the wine and stock and bring to the boil. Add the lemon rind and juice, with salt and pepper and pour over the chicken. Add the bay leaf.
4. Cover the casserole and cook in a preheated oven for about 40 minutes.
5. Blend the cream with the egg yolk, add some of the sauce from the casserole, then stir back into the casserole with the grapes. Replace the lid and return to the oven for 15 minutes.
6. Discard the bay leaf and serve garnished with small bunches of grapes or kiwi fruit slices and watercress.

Variation:
Turkey, pork or fish can also be used for this dish. For a fish Véronique, use either fillets of sole or plaice rolled up (allowing 2 per portion) and arranged in a shallow ovenproof dish. Make the sauce using the butter, flour, wine and 4 tablespoons milk in place of the stock and bring to the boil. Add lemon rind and juice, salt and pepper and 6 tablespoons double or single cream. Pour over the fish, cover and cook for 25 minutes. Add the grapes to the sauce, cover the casserole and return to the oven for a further 10-15 minutes. If using pork, cut 2 thick pork fillets into slices, about 4 cm (1½ inches) thick, and cook as for chicken. If using turkey, use 4 thick fillets or escalopes or thin slices of turkey rolled loosely and cook as for chicken.

Chicken with lemon and walnuts

4 chicken portions	*450 ml (¾ pint) beef stock*
salt	*1 tablespoon black treacle*
freshly ground black pepper	*grated rind of 1 lemon*
40 g (1½ oz) butter or	*2 tablespoons lemon juice*
margarine	*50 g (2 oz) walnut pieces*
2 tablespoons chopped spring	*To garnish:*
onions	*julienne strips of lemon rind*
1 tablespoon flour	*walnut halves*
1 teaspoon ground ginger	*parsley sprigs*

Preparation time: *20 minutes*
Cooking time: *1 hour*
Oven: *180°C, 350°F, Gas Mark 4*

1. Sprinkle the chicken with salt and pepper. Melt the fat in a pan and fry the chicken until browned all over. Transfer to a casserole.
2. Fry the onions in the same fat until soft. Stir in the flour and ginger and cook for 1 minute. Gradually add the stock and bring to the boil for 1 minute.
3. Stir in the black treacle, lemon rind, juice and walnuts. Pour over the chicken and cover the casserole.
4. Cook in a preheated oven for 1 hour. Spoon off any excess fat from the surface and adjust the seasoning.
5. Garnish with lemon rind, walnuts and parsley.

Chicken rollups

4 boneless chicken breasts,	*1 onion peeled and sliced*
skinned and beaten	*25 g (1 oz) flour*
salt	*300 ml (½ pint) chicken stock*
freshly ground black pepper	*4 tablespoons medium sherry*
175-225 g (6-8 oz) smoked	*100 g (4 oz) button mushrooms,*
pork sausage	*thickly sliced*
25 g (1 oz) butter or margarine	*12 stuffed green olives, halved*
1 tablespoon oil	*parsley sprigs, to garnish*

Preparation time: *15 minutes*
Cooking time: *1 hour*
Oven: *180°C, 350°F, Gas Mark 4*

1. Sprinkle chicken with salt and pepper.
2. Trim the ends from the pork sausage and cut off 4 pieces, each weighing about 40 g (1½ oz). Slice the remainder and reserve for garnish. Place a piece of sausage on each piece of chicken, roll up and secure with wooden cocktail sticks.
3. Melt the fat and oil in a pan and fry the chicken rolls until browned all over. Transfer to a casserole.
4. Fry the onion in the same fat until lightly browned. Stir in the flour and cook for 1 minute. Gradually add the stock and sherry and bring to the boil. Add salt and pepper, the mushrooms and olives and pour the mixture over the chicken.
5. Cover and cook for 50-60 minutes or until tender.
6. Garnish with sausage and sprigs of parsley.

LEFT TO RIGHT: Chicken rollups; Pot roast boned turkey

Pot roast boned turkey

Serves 6-8

3.25 kg (7½ lb) oven-ready turkey, half-boned	*100 g (4 oz) fresh breadcrumbs*
25 g (1 oz) butter	*100 g (4 oz) smooth liver pâté*
150 ml (¼ pint) red wine	*1 teaspoon ground coriander*
225 g (8 oz) button mushrooms, chopped	*1 teaspoon dried mixed herbs*
Stuffing:	*salt*
25 g (1 oz) butter	*freshly ground black pepper*
1 onion, peeled and finely chopped	*Beurre manié:*
1 garlic clove, crushed (optional)	*25 g (1 oz) butter*
	25 g (1 oz) flour
3 sticks celery, finely chopped	*To garnish:*
	potato crisps
	watercress

Preparation time: *30-45 minutes*
Cooking time: *about 1½ hours*
Oven: *180°C, 350°F, Gas Mark 4*

Either ask your butcher to bone out the turkey or try it yourself. It can either be completely boned or have the lower leg [drumstick] and lower wing bones left in place, which helps balance the joint during cooking and whilst you serve.

1. To make the stuffing, melt 25 g (1 oz) of the butter in a pan and fry the onion, garlic and celery for 2-3 minutes. Turn into a bowl. Add the remaining ingredients and mix well.
2. Spread the stuffing over the inside of the turkey and pull the flesh over to cover it. Secure with small skewers or sew together with string.
3. Turn the turkey over and shape evenly; position the legs and wings and truss loosely.
4. Heat the remaining butter and fry the turkey to brown lightly all over. Transfer to a casserole.
5. Add the wine to the pan drippings and bring to the boil. Add salt and pepper and pour the mixture over the turkey. Cover the casserole.
6. Cook in a preheated oven for 1 hour.
7. Baste the joint thoroughly, cover again and return to the oven for a further 30 minutes or until the juices run clear when the turkey is pierced deeply with a skewer.
8. Remove the joint and keep warm. Bring the pan juices back to the boil and add the mushrooms. Cream the butter and flour together to make beurre manié, then whisk into the sauce a little at a time and bring back to the boil for 2 minutes.
9. Stand the turkey on a serving dish and garnish with potato crisps and watercress. Serve the sauce separately in a sauceboat.

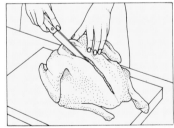

Remove parson's nose. Cut along backbone with sharp knife.

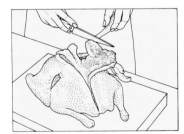

Cut flesh from body to wing. Cut through socket joint.

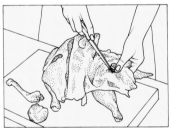

Scrape flesh off bone to next joint; break; remove bone.

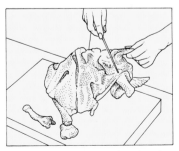

Cut flesh from carcass to leg; break joint; remove top bone.

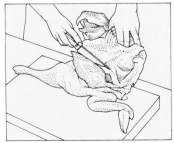

Carefully cut breast flesh from one side of breast bone.

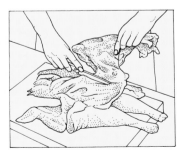

Repeat with other side of breast bone. Remove carcass.

Wild duck in Cumberland sauce

2 wild duck	4 tablespoons port
salt	3 tablespoons redcurrant, cranberry or bramble jelly
freshly ground black pepper	
25 g (1 oz) melted butter	1 tablespoon cornflour
finely pared rind of 1 orange and 1 lemon	To garnish: orange slices
juice of 2 oranges	watercress
juice of ½-1 lemon	

Preparation time: *about 15 minutes*
Cooking time: *about 1¼ hours*
Oven: *220°C, 425°F, Gas Mark 7; 180°C, 350°F, Gas Mark 4*

1. Place the ducks in a large casserole, sprinkle with salt and pepper and brush with melted butter. Cook uncovered in a preheated oven for 20 minutes, basting once.
2. Meanwhile cut the fruit rinds into julienne strips and cook in boiling water for 5 minutes; drain.
3. Heat the fruit juices, port and redcurrant jelly until the jelly melts. Add most of the fruit rinds and some salt and pepper.
4. Spoon off any fat from the ducks, leaving just the pan juices, and pour the orange mixture over the birds. Cover the casserole with a lid or foil.
5. Reduce the oven temperature and cook the ducks for about 45 minutes, basting once or twice, until tender.
6. Strain off the juices from the ducks into a saucepan and add the cornflour, blended in a little cold water. Bring to the boil until thickened and adjust the seasoning. Serve in a jug.
7. Serve the ducks on a large plate, sprinkled with the reserved strips of fruit rind and garnished with orange slices and watercress.

> The easiest way to remove rind without the white pith from citrus fruit is with a potato peeler; simply use as if peeling a potato. Otherwise cut the rind as thinly as possible with a sharp knife, then place on a flat surface, rind side downwards, and cut off all the white pith. Julienne strips are very narrow strips which are easily cut with a large heavy sharp knife.

Turkey escalopes in creamed corn

4 turkey escalopes	Stuffing:
salt	50 g (2 oz) butter or margarine
freshly ground black pepper	½ onion, peeled and finely chopped
25 g (1 oz) butter or margarine	
1 onion, peeled and thinly sliced	1 stick celery, finely chopped
	50 g (2 oz) fresh breadcrumbs
1 garlic clove, peeled and crushed	grated rind and juice of 1 orange
about 150 ml (¼ pint) chicken stock	8 stuffed green olives, chopped
2 teaspoons flour	To garnish:
1 × 275 g (10 oz) can cream style sweetcorn	orange slices
	stuffed green olives
	watercress

Preparation time: *20 minutes*
Cooking time: *about 40 minutes*
Oven: *180°C, 350°F, Gas Mark 4*

1. Beat the turkey escalopes between 2 sheets of cling film or damp greaseproof paper until thin enough to roll up. Sprinkle lightly with salt and pepper.
2. For the stuffing, melt the butter in a pan and fry the onion and celery until soft. Mix with the breadcrumbs, half the orange rind, stuffed olives and salt and pepper.
3. Divide between the pieces of turkey and roll up or fold in 3 to enclose the stuffing. Secure with wooden cocktail sticks.
4. Melt the butter in the pan and fry the turkey rolls or parcels until golden brown; transfer to a shallow casserole.
5. Fry the onion and garlic in the remaining fat in the pan until golden brown.
6. Make the orange juice up to 225 ml (8 fl oz) with stock.
7. Stir the flour into the pan and cook for 1 minute, then gradually add the orange stock and bring to the boil. Stir in the remaining orange rind and the creamed corn and bring back to the boil. Season with salt and pepper and pour over the turkey.
8. Cover the casserole with a lid or foil and cook in a preheated oven for about 40 minutes.
9. Serve garnished with orange slices, stuffed olives and watercress.

TOP TO BOTTOM: Wild duck in Cumberland sauce; Turkey escalopes in creamed corn

Chicken breasts in quince sauce

3 quinces, peeled, cored and sliced	4 rashers streaky bacon, derinded and chopped
300 ml (½ pint) water	1 tablespoon flour
4 boneless chicken breasts	1 chicken stock cube
salt	sprigs of fresh herbs, to garnish
freshly ground black pepper	(optional)
25 g (1 oz) butter or margarine	
1 tablespoon oil	
1 onion, peeled and chopped	

Preparation time: *20 minutes*
Cooking time: *about 45 minutes*
Oven: *180°C, 350°F, Gas Mark 4*

For those who prefer dark chicken meat, use 8 pieces of chicken thigh meat in place of the breasts.

1. Cook the quinces in a covered small pan with the water for 15 minutes or until beginning to soften.
2. Trim the chicken and sprinkle with salt and pepper. Heat the fat and oil in pan and fry the chicken until browned all over. Remove to a casserole.
3. Fry the onion and bacon gently in the fat left in the pan, until lightly coloured.
4. Stir the flour into the pan and cook for 1 minute. Drain the juice from the quinces and make up to 300 ml (½ pint) with water. Add to the pan with the stock cube and bring to the boil.
5. Stir the quinces into the sauce, add salt and pepper and pour over the chicken.
6. Cover the casserole and cook in a preheated oven for about 45 minutes or until tender. Garnish with sprigs of fresh herbs (optional).

CLOCKWISE FROM THE TOP: Duck with olives; Venison steaks with juniper berries; Chicken breasts in quince sauce

Duck with olives

4 duck portions (preferably wings), about 300-425 g (11-15 oz) each	150 ml (¼ pint) chicken stock
	6 tablespoons medium sherry
salt	2 tablespoons lemon juice
freshly ground black pepper	grated rind of ½ lemon
1 tablespoon oil	12-16 stuffed green olives, halved
1 onion, peeled and thinly sliced	To garnish:
	lemon slices or wedges
1 tablespoon flour	parsley sprigs (optional)

Preparation time: *15 minutes*
Cooking time: *about 1 hour*
Oven: *180°C, 350°F, Gas Mark 4*

1. Trim any excess fat from the duck portions and prick the skin with a fork. Sprinkle with salt and pepper.
2. Heat the oil in a pan and fry the duck until well browned all over, then transfer to a casserole. Pour off all but 1 tablespoon of the fat from the pan.
3. Fry the onion in the same fat until soft, then stir in the flour and cook for 1 minute.
4. Gradually add the stock, sherry and lemon juice and bring to the boil for 2 minutes. Add the lemon rind and the olives, season with salt and pepper and pour over the duck.
5. Cover the casserole and cook in a preheated oven for 50-60 minutes, until very tender, basting once during cooking.
6. Spoon off the excess fat from the surface of the casserole and garnish with lemon and parsley (if using).

> Duck portions are available in supermarkets both fresh and frozen and these are ideal. The wing portions are larger and more meaty and thus more expensive than the legs. A whole duck can also be used if it is cut into portions using poultry shears, sharp kitchen scissors or a sharp knife. A part thawed duck will be easier to cut into portions but make sure that all portions are fully thawed before cooking both for safety and to ensure against the duck being tough.

Venison steaks with juniper berries

4 venison steaks, about 175 g (6 oz) each	1 tablespoon wine vinegar
	2 tablespoons cranberry sauce or jelly
salt	
freshly ground black pepper	3 tablespoons double cream
25 g (1 oz) butter or margarine	1½ teaspoons cornflour
juice and grated rind of ½ lemon	To garnish:
	carrot and celery sticks
12 juniper berries, crushed	watercress (optional)
200 ml (7 fl oz) beef stock	

Preparation time: *15 minutes*
Cooking time: *about 50 minutes*
Oven: *200°C, 400°F, Gas Mark 6*

1. Trim the steaks if necessary and sprinkle with salt and pepper.
2. Melt the butter in a pan and when really hot add the steaks and fry to seal on both sides. Transfer to a casserole.
3. Add the lemon juice and rind to the pan juices with the juniper berries, stock, vinegar and cranberry sauce or jelly. Bring to the boil and boil rapidly for 2-3 minutes, making sure the residue in the pan is well mixed in. Season well.
4. Pour the sauce off the steaks and cover. Cook in a preheated oven for 40 minutes.
5. Pour the sauce off the steaks into a small pan. Keep the meat covered and warm. Blend the cream with the cornflour, then add a little of the sauce. Pour it all back into the pan and bring to the boil for 1 minute. Adjust the seasoning.
6. Arrange the steaks in a deep serving dish, pour the sauce over and garnish with carrot and celery sticks and sprigs of watercress (if using).

Variation:
Since venison is often rather difficult to obtain, try using four 2.5 cm (1 inch) thick rump steaks as an alternative

Poulet en cocotte Basquais

Serves 4-6

1.75 kg (4 lb) chicken	1 red pepper, deseeded and sliced
salt	
freshly ground black pepper	1 × 425 g (15 oz) can tomatoes
2 tablespoons oil or dripping	150 ml (¼ pint) white wine or stock
2 onions, peeled and thickly sliced	
	75 g (3 oz) sliced salami
1 garlic clove, peeled and crushed	1 bay leaf
	parsley sprigs, to garnish

Preparation time: *15 minutes*
Cooking time: *1½ hours*
Oven: *180°C, 350°F, Gas Mark 4*

1. Wipe the chicken inside and out. Chop the liver but discard the rest of the giblets. Sprinkle the bird all over with salt and pepper. Heat the oil or dripping in a pan and fry the chicken until browned all over. Transfer to a large casserole.
2. Fry the onions, garlic and pepper for a few minutes until softening, then add the chicken liver, tomatoes and wine or stock. Bring to the boil.
3. Chop 50 g (2 oz) of the salami and add to the pan with salt and pepper and the bay leaf. Spoon the vegetable mixture around the chicken and pour over the liquid. Cover the casserole tightly.
4. Cook in a preheated oven for 1½ hours or until the chicken is tender.
5. Discard the bay leaf and serve the chicken garnished with the remaining slices of salami and the sprigs of parsley.

Variation:
This is a country way of serving chicken, baked whole in a heavy pot along with salami, peppers, tomatoes and garlic; once prepared and in the oven it can be forgotten until ready to serve. It goes well with boiled or creamed potatoes or boiled rice and a green vegetable/or green salad. Any leftover chicken can be served cold; the flavour is superb. To serve large numbers, a much larger chicken or small turkey — say up to 3.2-3.5 kg (7-8 lb) can be used; simply increase the cooking time to about 2½ hours or until quite tender when tested with a skewer. If you haven't a large enough casserole for a larger bird use a roasting tin and cover tightly and securely with foil before cooking.

Pigeons with black cherries

4 pigeons	2 tablespoons wine vinegar
salt	2 tablespoons brandy
freshly ground black pepper	1-2 sprigs fresh thyme
2 tablespoons oil	Fleurons:
175 g (6 oz) pickling onions, peeled	100 g (4 oz) puff pastry
	milk or beaten egg, to glaze
2 tablespoons flour	chopped fresh thyme, to garnish (optional)
1 × 425 g (15 oz) can black cherries	
about 150 ml (¼ pint) beef stock	

Preparation time: *15 minutes*
Cooking time: *about 1½ hours*
Oven: *160°C, 325°F, Gas Mark 3;*
200°C, 400°F, Gas Mark 6

1. Halve the pigeons and remove the backbone, using a pair of poultry shears, kitchen scissors or a sharp knife. Sprinkle the birds with salt and pepper.
2. Heat the oil in a pan and fry the pieces until lightly browned. Transfer to a casserole.
3. Fry the onions in the same fat until lightly browned. Stir in the flour and cook for 1 minute.
4. Drain juices from the cherries and make up to 450 ml (¾ pint) with stock. Gradually add to the pan and bring to the boil. Add the cherries and season with salt and pepper.
5. Add the wine vinegar, brandy and thyme and pour over the pigeons. Cover the casserole.
6. Cook in a preheated oven for about 1½ hours or until the pigeons are very tender.
7. To make the pastry fleurons, roll out the puff pastry and cut into 7 cm (2½ inch) crescents, using a fluted pastry cutter. Stand on a baking sheet, brush with milk or beaten egg and cook in a preheated oven at the higher temperature for about 10-15 minutes until golden brown. Cool on a wire tray.
8. Discard the sprigs of thyme and serve garnished with pastry fleurons and sprinkled with chopped fresh thyme (if using).

Variation:
Use 4 partridges instead of the pigeons and leave them whole.

CLOCKWISE FROM THE LEFT: Poulet en cocotte Basquais; Pigeons with black cherries; Coconut chicken

Coconut chicken

4 tablespoons desiccated coconut	2 sticks celery, sliced
150 ml (¼ pint) boiling water	2 tablespoons flour
4 chicken portions	300 ml (½ pint) chicken stock
salt	few strands of saffron or ¼ teaspoon turmeric
freshly ground black pepper	½ teaspoon ground coriander
25 g (1 oz) butter or margarine	To garnish:
1 tablespoon oil	toasted strands of shredded coconut
1 onion, peeled and sliced	parsley sprigs
1 garlic clove, peeled and crushed	

Preparation time: *20 minutes*
Cooking time: *1 hour*
Oven: *180°C, 350°F, Gas Mark 4*

1. Put the coconut into a small bowl, pour on the water, mix well and leave to stand for 10 minutes.
2. Trim the chicken portions and sprinkle with salt and pepper. Heat the butter and oil in a pan and fry chicken until well browned. Transfer to a casserole.
3. Fry the onion, garlic and celery gently in the same fat until soft. Stir in the flour and cook for 1 minute.
4. Add the stock followed by the coconut mixture and bring to the boil. Stir in the saffron or turmeric, coriander and salt and pepper and pour over the chicken.
5. Cover the casserole and cook in a preheated oven for 1 hour until tender.
6. Spoon off any excess fat from the surface of the casserole and garnish with toasted shredded coconut and parsley.

Variation:
When fresh coconuts are available, replace the desiccated coconut and water with 150 ml (¼ pint) coconut milk and add about 50 g (2 oz) freshly grated coconut to the sauce.

Festive pheasant with chestnuts

4 pheasant breasts or joints	1 tablespoon redcurrant jelly
salt	rind of 1 orange, cut into
freshly ground black pepper	julienne strips
25 g (1 oz) butter	juice of 2 oranges
1 tablespoon oil	2 tablespoons brandy
225 g (8 oz) button onions,	(optional)
peeled	1 bay leaf
225-350 g (8-12 oz) chestnuts,	To garnish:
lightly roasted or boiled and	orange slices
peeled	watercress
2 tablespoons flour	potato crisps or matchsticks
200 ml (7 fl oz) dry white wine	(optional)
150 ml (¼ pint) chicken stock	

Preparation time: *15 minutes*
Cooking time: *50-60 minutes*
Oven: *180°C, 350°F, Gas Mark 4*

1. Sprinkle the pheasant with salt and pepper. Heat the butter and oil in a pan and fry the pieces until browned all over. Transfer to a casserole.

2. Fry the onions in the same fat until lightly coloured and arrange around the pheasant with the chestnuts.
3. Stir the flour into the fat remaining in the pan and cook for 1 minute. Gradually add the wine and stock and bring to the boil. Stir in the redcurrant jelly, orange rind and juice, the brandy (if using) and bay leaf. Add salt and pepper and pour over the pheasant.
4. Cover the casserole tightly and cook in a preheated oven for about 50-60 minutes or until tender.
5. Discard the bay leaf and serve the pheasant pieces on a platter surrounded by onions and chestnuts with some sauce spooned over and the rest served separately. Garnish with orange slices and watercress and, if liked, potato crisps or matchsticks.

Nick shell; boil 25 minutes.   *Use sharp knife to peel.*

Pot roast partridges with grapes

4 partridges, prepared	300 ml (½ pint) beef stock
salt	100-175 g (4-6 oz) green
freshly ground black pepper	grapes, halved and seeded
25 g (1 oz) butter or margarine	1 tablespoon cornflour
100 g (4 oz) streaky bacon	To garnish:
rashers, derinded and chopped	orange slices, cut in half
2 tablespoons brandy	green grapes
2 tablespoons medium sherry	
juice of 1 orange	

Preparation time: *15 minutes*
Cooking time: *1¼-1½ hours*
Oven: *180°C, 350°F, Gas Mark 4*

1. Sprinkle the birds with salt and pepper, melt the fat in a pan, then brown the partridges all over. Transfer to a casserole.
2. Fry the bacon in the same fat until golden brown, then stir in the brandy, sherry, orange juice and stock and bring to the boil. Season with salt and pepper and pour over the partridges.
3. Cover the casserole and cook in a preheated oven for 1 hour, basting once.
4. Add the grapes to the casserole and return to the oven for 15-30 minutes or until quite tender.
5. Drain off the juices into a pan and skim off most of the fat. Blend the cornflour with a little cold water and add to the sauce. Bring back to the boil, adjust the seasoning and pour back over the partridges.
6. Garnish with halved orange slices and green grapes.

Variation:

When partridges are not available, pigeons, which are much easier to obtain, can be used; or use poussins if you would rather not use game at all. Pigeons may require about 30 minutes longer cooking and poussins 15-20 minutes less. A whole 1.75 kg (4 lb) chicken can also be pot roasted in the same way using this recipe; cooking time should be 1½-1¾ hours.

LEFT TO RIGHT: Festive pheasant with chestnuts; Pot roast partridges with grapes

FISH

Haddock and prawn cobbler

550 g (1¼ lb) haddock fillet, skinned and cut into 5 × 2.5 cm (2 × 1 inch) pieces
100 g (4 oz) peeled prawns
25 g (1 oz) butter or margarine
25 g (1 oz) flour
300 ml (½ pint) milk
salt
freshly ground black pepper
2 teaspoons dry mustard
1 tablespoon wine vinegar
2 hard-boiled eggs, quartered.

Scone topping:
175 g (6 oz) granary flour
1 tablespoon baking powder
½ teaspoon dried thyme (optional)
40 g (1½ oz) butter or margarine
1 egg, beaten
about 2 tablespoons milk
To garnish:
whole prawns
parsley sprigs

Preparation time: 15 minutes
Cooking time: about 45 minutes
Oven: 180°C, 350°F, Gas Mark 4;
200°C, 400°F, Gas Mark 6

1. Place the fish in a lightly greased, shallow casserole with the peeled prawns.
2. Melt the fat in a pan, stir in the flour and cook for 1 minute. Gradually add the milk and bring to the boil for 1 minute. Add salt and pepper, mustard and vinegar, then pour over the fish.
3. Cover the casserole and cook in a preheated oven for 25 minutes. Remove the lid, add the eggs and give the fish a stir to mix evenly.
4. Meanwhile to make the scones, mix the flour, baking powder and thyme (if using) together with a little salt and pepper and rub in the fat. Add the egg and sufficient milk to make a softish dough. Turn on to a floured surface.
5. Roll or pat the dough out to about 1 cm (½ inch) thick and cut into 4-5 cm (1½-2 inch) triangles or squares. Arrange round the edge of the casserole over the fish and brush with milk.
6. Increase the oven temperature and return the casserole, uncovered, to the oven for about 20 minutes or until the scones are well risen and browned. Serve garnished with whole prawns and parsley.

Squid Provençal

1.5 kg (3 lb) fresh squid
2 tablespoons olive oil
2 onions, peeled and sliced
1 garlic clove, peeled and crushed
2 tablespoons flour
1 tablespoon tomato purée
200 ml (7 fl oz) dry white wine or vermouth
150 ml (¼ pint) stock
1 tablespoon lemon juice

350 g (12 oz) tomatoes, peeled and sliced
salt
freshly ground black pepper
½ teaspoon paprika
pinch of cayenne
pinch of sugar
1 bay leaf
chopped fresh parsley, to garnish

Preparation time: 20-25 minutes
Cooking time: about 45 minutes
Oven: 160°C, 325°F, Gas Mark 3

1. To prepare the squid, pull the head part firmly away from the bag and remove 'nib'. Remove red skin from body, wash and cut into rings. Cut the tentacles into pieces. Discard the head and entrails.
2. Heat the oil in a flameproof casserole and fry the onions and garlic until lightly browned. Add the squid and cook until lightly coloured.
3. Stir in the flour followed by the tomato purée, wine or vermouth, stock and lemon juice. Bring to the boil and add the tomatoes, salt and pepper, paprika, cayenne and sugar to taste. Add the bay leaf and cover.
4. Cook in a preheated oven for about 45 minutes or until tender. Discard the bay leaf and adjust the seasoning. Serve garnished with chopped parsley.

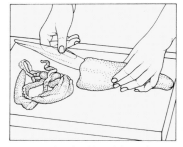

TOP TO BOTTOM: Haddock and prawn cobbler; Squid Provencal

Pull head away from bag.

Remove hard 'nib' and discard.

Somerset haddock

675 g (1½ lb) haddock fillets, skinned	25 g (1 oz) flour
salt	300 ml (½ pint) dry or medium cider
freshly ground black pepper	1 tablespoon chopped fresh chives or 1 teaspoon dried chives
3 tomatoes, peeled, quartered and deseeded	
175 g (6 oz) mushrooms or apples, sliced	¼ teaspoon grated lemon rind
25 g (1 oz) butter or margarine	1 tablespoon lemon juice

Preparation time: *10 minutes*
Cooking time: *45 minutes*
Oven: *180°C, 350°F, Gas Mark 4*

1. Cut the fish into 4 equal portions, sprinkle lightly with salt and pepper and fold up. Place in a shallow ovenproof casserole, Arrange the tomatoes and mushrooms or apples over the fish.
2. Melt the butter in a pan, stir in the flour and cook for 1 minute. Gradually add the cider and bring to the boil, stirring frequently. Add the chives, lemon rind and juice and season with salt and pepper.
3. Pour over the fish and cover with a lid or foil.
4. Cook in a preheated oven for about 45 minutes or until the fish is cooked through. Drain the juices from the casserole into a saucepan and keep the casserole warm. Reduce the sauce by about one third, pour it over the fish and serve.

Bouillabaisse

1.25 kg (2½ lb) mixed fish and shellfish	salt and freshly ground black pepper
6 tablespoons oil	grated rind of ½ lemon
2 large onions, peeled and thinly sliced	juice of 1 lemon
2 sticks celery, thinly sliced	pinch of saffron or turmeric
2 carrots, peeled and diced	about 300 ml (½ pint) white wine
2 garlic cloves, peeled and crushed	To garnish:
450 g (1 lb) tomatoes, peeled and sliced	chopped fresh parsley and/or mixed fresh herbs
1 bouquet garni	few whole prawns or crayfish

Preparation time: *20 minutes*
Cooking time: *about 50 minutes*
Oven: *180°C, 350°F, Gas Mark 4*

A true bouillabaisse is made using at least 8 types of fish and shellfish but many of the authentic types are only available in Mediterranean areas. Your fishmonger should help with a good selection if you explain your requirements.

1. Clean the fish, remove all the skin and any loose bones, wash and cut into pieces about 5 cm (2 inches). Remove the shellfish from the shells, except for prawns or crayfish for garnish, and wash thoroughly.
2. Heat the oil in a pan and fry the onions, celery, carrots and garlic gently, until soft but only lightly coloured.
3. Add the tomatoes, bouquet garni, salt, pepper, lemon rind, juice and saffron or turmeric and turn into a casserole.
4. Lay the fish over the vegetables, then add enough wine almost to cover the fish.
5. Cover the casserole and cook in a preheated oven for about 50 minutes, until the fish is tender. Discard the bouquet garni and taste and adjust the seasoning.
6. Serve very hot, sprinkled with chopped parsley and/or fresh herbs and a few whole prawns or crayfish. Accompany with crusty bread or boiled rice.

CLOCKWISE FROM THE TOP LEFT: Somerset haddock; Braised salmon steaks with asparagus; Scallops Felix; Bouillabaisse

When fresh scallops are unavailable use frozen ones but make sure they are completetely thawed before commencing.

1. Remove any black pieces from the scallops and wash. Cut the roes from the scallops and cut the white part into 2 or 3 pieces depending on size. Place in a casserole with the bouquet garni.
2. Bring the wine, stock or water, salt, pepper and lemon juice to the boil, pour over the scallops and cover. Cook in a preheated oven for 20 minutes or until nearly tender.
3. Meanwhile melt the fat in a pan and fry the onion and celery gently, until soft but not coloured.
4. Drain the cooking liquid from the scallops and reserve. Discard the bouquet garni.
5. Stir the flour into the onions and cook for 1 minute. Gradually add the scallop liquid and bring to the boil for 2 minutes. Add salt and pepper, the mushrooms, cream and Tabasco and pour back over the scallops.
6. Combine the breadcrumbs and cheese and sprinkle over. Increase the oven temperature and cook for about 20 minutes or until the top is crisp and brown. Serve at once, garnished with cucumber and lemon.

Braised salmon steaks with asparagus

4 salmon steaks, about 2.5 cm (1 inch) thick	2 teaspoons cornflour
salt	6 tablespoons double cream
freshly ground black pepper	2 teaspoons lemon juice
1 × 350 g (12 oz) can asparagus	lemon wedges, to garnish

Preparation time: *10 minutes*
Cooking time: *40 minutes*
Oven: *190°C, 375°F, Gas Mark 5*

1. Place the fish in a shallow, buttered ovenproof dish just large enough to take the steaks in a single layer. Sprinkle with salt and pepper.
2. Drain the asparagus, reserving 6 tablespoons of the liquid. Reserve 12 asparagus spears for garnish and roughly chop the remainder. Scatter over the fish.
3. Blend the cornflour with the cream and then with the asparagus liquid, lemon juice and season with salt and pepper. Pour over the fish.
4. Cover and cook in a preheated oven for about 40 minutes or until the fish is cooked through. The cooking time depends on the thickness of the fish.
5. Garnish with the reserved asparagus and lemon wedges.

Scallops Felix

10-12 scallops	175 g (6 oz) button mushrooms, quartered or sliced
1 bouquet garni	
150 ml (¼ pint) white wine	3 tablespoons double or soured cream
150 ml (¼ pint) chicken stock or water	few drops of Tabasco sauce
salt	50 g (2 oz) fresh white breadcrumbs
freshly ground black pepper	
1 tablespoon lemon juice	25 g (1 oz) mature Cheddar cheese, finely grated
40 g (1½ oz) butter or margarine	cucumber and lemon slices, to garnish
1 large onion, peeled and finely chopped	
2-3 sticks celery, thinly sliced	
25 g (1 oz) flour	

Preparation time: *10 minutes*
Cooking time: *about 40 minutes*
Oven: *180°C, 350°F, Gas Mark 4;*
220°C, 425°F, Gas Mark 7

Plaice paupiettes with smoked salmon

4 plaice (about 350 g (12 oz) each) filleted	150 ml (¼ pint) dry white wine
salt	300 ml (½ pint) milk
freshly ground black pepper	3 tablespoons single cream
100 g (4 oz) smoked salmon	1 tablespoon lemon juice
40 g (1½ oz) butter or margarine	To garnish:
	8 whole prawns
40 g (1½ oz) flour	sprigs of parsley, fennel or dill (optional)

Preparation time: *20 minutes*
Cooking time: *50 minutes*
Oven: *180°C, 350°F, Gas Mark 4*

1. Wipe the 8 plaice fillets and sprinkle lightly with salt and pepper. Divide the smoked salmon into 8 pieces and lay 1 piece on the skin side of each fillet. Roll up loosely towards the tail and place the fillets in a lightly greased, shallow ovenproof dish.
2. Melt the butter or margarine in a pan, stir in the flour and cook for 1 minute. Gradually add the wine, followed by the milk and bring to the boil for 2 minutes. Season with salt and pepper, stir in the cream and lemon juice and pour the sauce over the fish.
3. Cover the dish with foil or a lid and cook in a preheated oven for about 50 minutes or until cooked through.
4. Remove the foil and garnish the plaice rolls with whole prawns and parsley, fennel or dill (if using).

Variation:
Fillets of sole (particularly slip or lemon sole) may be used instead of plaice.

Plaice fillets can be used with the skins on but if you prefer to remove them, it is quite simple to do. Place on a wooden board or working surface and, using a sharp knife, begin at the tail and carefully run the knife along towards the head, keeping the blade slanting downwards and working away from you. The fillet will then easily lift away from the skin. If you work from the head to the tail the flesh will crumble up and break and will not come away from the skin in one piece. If the fish slips sprinkle a little coarse salt on the surface before you begin; rinse the fillets before cooking to remove any salt.

Mussels in cider

4.5 litres (4 quarts) fresh mussels	1 tablespoon lemon juice
50 g (2 oz) butter	salt
2 onions, peeled and finely chopped	freshly ground black pepper
	2 bay leaves
2 carrots, peeled and finely chopped	4 teaspoons cornflour
	3 tablespoons double cream
1-2 garlic cloves, peeled and crushed	chopped fresh parsley, to garnish
450 ml (¾ pint) medium cider	

Preparation time: *20 minutes*
Cooking time: *about 20 minutes*
Oven: *200°C, 400°F, Gas Mark 6*

1. Wash and scrub the mussels in several bowls of cold water, making sure they are thoroughly clean. The water should be clear when they are ready. Discard any which rise to the top or those which are broken or do not close when given a sharp tap. Pull away beard; drain.
2. Melt the butter in a large flameproof casserole and fry the onions, carrots and garlic gently until soft but not coloured.
3. Add the cider and lemon juice and bring to the boil. Add salt, pepper and bay leaves.
4. Add the mussels and mix well. Cover the casserole tightly and cook in a preheated oven for about 20 minutes, or until the mussels have opened out. (Discard any which do not open.)
5. Blend the cornflour with the cream and stir into the sauce. Bring slowly to the boil and cook until slightly thickened.
6. Ladle the mussels and the sauce into large bowls and serve generously sprinkled with parsley and with plenty of fresh crusty bread.

Tap open mussels to close.

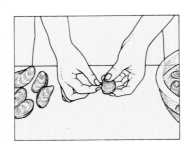

Pull away hairy beard.

Rainbow trout with brown butter and almonds

4 rainbow trout, cleaned	grated rind of ½ lemon
salt	25 g (1 oz) blanched almonds, finely chopped
freshly ground black pepper	
50 g (2 oz) butter	1 tablespoon chopped fresh parsley
50 g (2 oz) blanched almonds, roughly chopped	
	1 egg yolk
2 tablespoons lemon juice	To garnish:
Stuffing balls:	parsley sprigs
75 g (3 oz) fresh breadcrumbs	lemon wedges
2 tablespoons grated onion	

Preparation time: *15 minutes*
Cooking time: *about 45 minutes*
Oven: *160°C, 325°F, Gas Mark 3*

1. Lightly grease a casserole or ovenproof dish. Sprinkle the fish inside with salt and pepper and lay head to tail in the dish in a single layer.
2. Melt the butter in a pan and fry the almonds until lightly browned and the butter is also browning. Remove from the heat, stir in the lemon juice and pour quickly over the fish.
3. For the stuffing balls, place the breadcrumbs in a bowl with the onion, lemon rind, chopped nuts and parsley. Season with salt and pepper and bind together with the egg yolk.
4. Divide into 8, shape into balls and arrange round the fish.
5. Cover the dish with a lid or foil and cook in a preheated oven for about 45 minutes or until the fish are tender. Serve garnished with parsley and lemon wedges.

Trout are always served with their heads on, unless smoked. If you find this unappealing, cover the eye with a slice of stuffed olive or tiny sprig of parsley. Fish farms sell trout straight from their ponds; you simply state what you want and the fish are caught, killed and cleaned for you — they couldn't be fresher. Trout are also widely available from wet fish shops and are sold frozen too. One fish is sufficient for a portion.

Seafood casserole

Serves 6

450 g (1 lb) haddock or cod fillet, skinned	40 g (1½ oz) flour
225 g (8 oz) smoked haddock fillet, skinned	300 ml (½ pint) milk
100 g (4 oz) peeled prawns	1 teaspoon made English mustard
3-4 scallops, quartered or 1 × 150 g (5 oz) jar mussels, drained	1 tablespoon lemon juice
1 × 325 g (11 oz) can sweetcorn kernels, drained	4 tablespoons soured cream
1-2 canned red pimentos, sliced (optional)	salt
40 g (1½ oz) butter or margarine	freshly ground black pepper

1 teaspoon made English mustard
1 tablespoon lemon juice
4 tablespoons soured cream
salt
freshly ground black pepper
To garnish:
cooked peas (optional)
whole prawns

Preparation time: *10 minutes*
Cooking time: *40-45 minutes*
Oven: *180°C, 350°F, Gas Mark 4*

1. Cut the white and smoked fish into 2.5 cm (1 inch) cubes. Place in a large, fairly shallow casserole with the prawns, scallops or mussels, sweetcorn and pimentos (if using).
2. Melt the butter or margarine in a pan, stir in the flour and cook for 1 minute. Gradually add the milk and bring to the boil.
3. Stir the mustard, lemon juice, soured cream and salt and pepper into the sauce and pour into the casserole.
4. Cook in a preheated oven for about 40 minutes or until the fish is cooked through.
5. Give the casserole a gentle stir then spoon a layer of peas (if using) round the edge of the dish and garnish with whole prawns.

Variation:
Use all white fish in place of the smoked haddock and add 1-2 teaspoons anchovy essence to the sauce instead of the mustard. Anchovy fillets or prawns can be used alone for the garnish.

The milk can be replaced by 300 ml (½ pint) each of dry cider or dry white wine and chicken stock. A quick fish stock can be made by simmering the fish skins in 300 ml (½ pint) water flavoured with 1 peeled and sliced onion, 1 peeled and chopped carrot, 2 sprigs of parsley and a bay leaf. Bring to boil, then simmer gently for about 15 minutes – fast boiling results in a bitter stock. Strain and use in place of chicken stock.

TOP TO BOTTOM: Mussels in cider; Rainbow trout with brown butter and almonds; Seafood casserole

Fish paella

50 g (2 oz) butter	100-175 g (4-6 oz) crabmeat
1 tablespoon oil	(fresh, frozen or canned),
1 large onion, peeled and	roughly flaked
sliced	100 g (4 oz) peeled prawns
1-2 garlic cloves, peeled and	4-8 crayfish
crushed	2 bay leaves
1 medium red pepper,	600 ml (1 pint) chicken or fish
deseeded and thinly sliced	stock
1 medium green pepper,	pinch of saffron or $\frac{1}{2}$ teaspoon
deseeded and thinly sliced	turmeric
175 g (6 oz) long grain rice	salt
175 g (6 oz) mushrooms,	freshly ground black pepper
trimmed and thickly sliced	100 g (4 oz) frozen peas
1 sole, filleted and cut into	600 ml (1 pint) fresh mussels,
2.5 cm (1 inch) pieces	cleaned (optional)

Preparation time: *about 20 minutes*
Cooking time: *about 50 minutes*
Oven: *180°C, 350°F, Gas Mark 4*

1. Melt the butter and oil in a pan and fry the onion and garlic gently until soft. Add the peppers, and continue cooking for 3 minutes. Turn into a greased casserole.
2. Add the rice, mushrooms, sole, crabmeat, prawns, crayfish and bay leaves to the casserole.
3. Bring the stock to the boil, add the saffron or turmeric and salt and pepper and pour over the rice.
4. Cover and cook in a preheated oven for 40 minutes.
5. Give a gentle stir to the rice, add the peas and mussels (if using) and recover the casserole. Return to the oven for 10 minutes or until the mussels have opened. (Discard any which do not open). Serve very hot.

Halibut à la Grecque

4 halibut steaks	1 bay leaf
salt	6 tablespoons white wine
freshly ground black pepper	175 g (6 oz) button mushrooms,
2 tablespoons oil	trimmed
1 medium onion, peeled and	To garnish:
chopped	tomatoes
2 carrots, peeled and diced	chopped fresh mixed herbs
1 garlic clove, peeled and	
crushed	

Preparation time: *15 minutes*
Cooking time: *35-40 minutes*
Oven: *180°C, 350°F, Gas Mark 4*

1. Lay the halibut steaks in a lightly greased shallow ovenproof dish or casserole and season.
2. Heat the oil in a pan and fry the onion, carrots and garlic gently until soft but not coloured.

3. Add the bay leaf, wine and salt and pepper to taste. Bring to the boil for 1 minute. Cut any large mushrooms in half, then add them to the pan. Pour the mixture over the fish.
4. Cover the casserole and cook in a preheated oven for 35-40 minutes or until the fish is tender.
5. Discard the bay leaf and garnish with quarters or slices of tomato and sprinkle liberally with chopped herbs.

Scallop and artichoke medley

225 g (8 oz) Jerusalem	salt
artichokes	freshly ground black pepper
2 tablespoons lemon juice	2 tablespoons cornflour
50 g (2 oz) butter or margarine	3 tablespoons single or soured
1 large onion, peeled and	cream
sliced	1-2 canned red pimentos, sliced
12 scallops	(optional)
1 bay leaf	To garnish:
150 ml ($\frac{1}{4}$ pint) dry vermouth	croûtons
150 ml ($\frac{1}{4}$ pint) water	sprigs of parsley

Preparation time: *15 minutes*
Cooking time: *40 minutes*
Oven: *180°C, 350°F, Gas Mark 4*

1. Peel the artichokes and slice into a bowl of cold water containing 1 tablespoon of the lemon juice.
2. Melt the fat in a flameproof casserole and fry the onion gently until soft, then add the well drained artichokes and continue frying gently for 3-4 minutes.
3. Cut the scallops into 3 or 4 pieces and add to the pan with the bay leaf, vermouth, remaining lemon juice and water and bring to the boil. Add salt and pepper to taste.
4. Cover and cook in a preheated oven for 25 minutes.
5. Blend the cornflour with the cream, add a little of the scallop liquid and return to the casserole, mixing well. Add the strips of red pimento (if using), cover the casserole again and return to the oven for 15 minutes.
6. Garnish the casserole with croûtons and sprigs of parsley

CLOCKWISE FROM THE LEFT: Fish paella; Halibut or turbot Clarinda; Halibut à la Grecque

Halibut or turbot Clarinda

4 halibut or turbot steaks	*1 tablespoon lemon juice*
salt	*1 teaspoon Angostura bitters*
freshly ground black pepper	*100 g (4 oz) crabmeat (fresh,*
25 g (1 oz) butter	*frozen or canned), flaked*
1 tablespoon finely chopped	*To garnish:*
onion	*whole prawns*
25 g (1 oz) flour	*cucumber sticks*
300 ml (½ pint) milk	

Preparation time: *10 minutes*
Cooking time: *about 40 minutes*
Oven: *180°C, 350°F, Gas Mark 4*

The halibut or turbot in this recipe makes it a dish for special occasions.

1. Place the fish steaks in a lightly greased ovenproof dish and sprinkle with salt and pepper.
2. Melt the butter in a pan and fry the onion gently until soft. Stir in the flour and cook for 1 minute. Gradually add the milk and bring to the boil for 1 minute.
3. Stir the lemon juice, Angostura bitters, crabmeat, and salt and pepper into the sauce and pour the mixture over the fish.
4. Cover the casserole and cook in a preheated oven for about 40 minutes or until the fish is tender.
5. Transfer to a serving dish and garnish with whole prawns and cucumber sticks.

FLAVOURS FROM ABROAD

Pot roast colonial goose

Serves 6

2 kg (4½ lb) leg of lamb, boned	1 × 200 g (7 oz) can apricot
Stuffing	halves
25 g (1 oz) butter or margarine	1 × 200 g (7 oz) can prunes
1 onion, peeled and finely	1 egg yolk
chopped	Sauce:
2 sticks celery, finely chopped	150 ml (¼ pint) dry white wine
3 rashers bacon, derinded and	15 g (½ oz) melted butter
chopped	150 ml (¼ pint) beef stock
75 g (3 oz) cooked rice	1½ tablespoons cornflour
pinch of ground allspice	To garnish:
salt	courgettes, lightly cooked
freshly ground black pepper	sprigs of fresh rosemary or
	parsley

Preparation time: *25 minutes, plus marinating*
Cooking time: *about 2¼ hours*
Oven: *180°C, 350°F, Gas Mark 4*

1. For the stuffing, melt the fat in a pan and fry the onion, celery and bacon until lightly browned. Place in a bowl and add the cooked rice, allspice, salt and pepper.
2. Drain the apricots and prunes, reserving the juices. Chop about 4 apricots and 4 prunes and add to the stuffing; mix well and bind together with the egg yolk.
3. Use the stuffing to fill the bone cavity of the lamb and sew loosely back into shape, using a trussing needle and fine string or several skewers.
4. Place the joint in a casserole with the wine, cover and leave to marinate for several hours, turning once.
5. Brush the surface of the meat with melted butter and sprinkle with salt. Cover and cook in the marinade in a preheated oven for about 2¼ hours or until tender and cooked through. Baste once or twice during cooking and remove the casserole lid for the last 20-30 minutes to brown the joint.
6. Strain off the juices into a saucepan, remove any fat from the surface and add 150 ml (¼ pint) mixed apricot and prune juice and the stock. Thicken with the cornflour blended in a little cold water and bring back to the boil for about 2 minutes. Serve in a sauceboat.
7. Remove the string or skewers from the lamb and place on a serving dish. Garnish with the remaining apricots, prunes

and the courgettes, and sprigs of fresh rosemary or parsley. Serve with potatoes cooked in their skins, coated with butter and sprinkled with chopped parsley.

Hawaiian chicken

4 chicken portions	1 × 225 g (8 oz) can crushed
salt	pineapple
freshly ground black pepper	1 tablespoon soy sauce
25 g (1 oz) butter or margarine	1 green pepper, deseeded,
25 g (1 oz) flour	sliced and blanched
1 teaspoon ground ginger	3-4 pieces stem ginger,
150 ml (¼ pint) chicken stock	chopped
	1 tablespoon lemon juice

Preparation time: *15 minutes*
Cooking time: *1 hour*
Oven: *180°C, 350°F, Gas Mark 4*

1. Trim the chicken and sprinkle with salt and pepper. Melt the fat in a pan and fry the chicken until browned all over. Transfer to a casserole.
2. Stir the flour and ginger into the remaining fat in the pan and cook for 1 minute.
3. Gradually add the stock, crushed pineapple (and its juice) and soy sauce. Bring to the boil for 2 minutes.
4. Season with salt and pepper and pour the sauce over the chicken. Cover the casserole and cook in a preheated oven for 45 minutes.
5. Add the green pepper and stem ginger to the casserole and the lemon juice to sharpen. Adjust the seasoning, cover the casserole again and return to the oven for 15 minutes or until tender.

Pot roast colonial goose

70

Boeuf en daube

Serves 5-6

1 kg (2 lb) best braising steak in a piece, cut into 5 cm (2 inch) pieces	2 carrots, peeled and sliced
	2 onions, peeled and sliced
1 garlic clove, peeled and crushed	450 ml (³⁄₄ pint) beef stock
	salt
1 tablespoon chopped fresh parsley	freshly ground black pepper
	2-3 slices smoked cooked ham, diced
1 teaspoon dried thyme	1 bay leaf
4 tablespoons brandy	chopped fresh parsley, to garnish
150 ml (¼ pint) dry white wine	
3 tablespoons oil	

Preparation time: _20 minutes, plus marinating_
Cooking time: _about 3½ hours_
Oven: _150°C, 300°F, Gas Mark 2_

1. Place the meat in a bowl. Add the garlic, parsley, thyme and brandy and mix well. Leave to stand for 15 minutes.
2. Add the wine, cover and leave to marinate for about 2 hours, turning the meat at least once.
3. Drain the meat, reserving the marinade, heat the oil in a pan and fry to seal, then place in a casserole.
4. Add the carrots and onions to the same fat and fry for 2 minutes. Add the marinade and stock: bring to the boil.
5. Add salt and pepper, the ham and bay leaf and place the contents of the pan in the casserole.
6. Cover tightly and cook in a preheated oven for about 3½ hours or until the beef is tender.
7. Discard the bay leaf, adjust the seasoning and serve sprinkled thickly with chopped parsley.

Variation:

This casserole is a classic French dish using steak in a piece; however, pieces of chicken or turkey taste very good when cooked in the same way. Allow 1 large chicken quarter or 2 smaller portions of chicken per person or a turkey thigh joint either with or without the bone. Cook for about 1¼-1½ hours or until the meat is very tender. Red wine may be used in place of white.

Chicken gumbo

25 g (1 oz) butter or margarine	2 tablespoons tomato purée
1.75 g (4 lb) chicken, cut into 8 pieces	2 teaspoons Worcestershire sauce
2 tablespoons oil	pinch of ground cloves
1 large onion, peeled and sliced	pinch of chilli powder
1 garlic clove, peeled and crushed	¼ teaspoon dried basil
	salt
1 green pepper, deseeded and sliced	freshly ground black pepper
1 tablespoon flour	To garnish:
1 × 425 g (15 oz) can tomatoes	225 g (8 oz) long grain rice, cooked
300 ml (½ pint) chicken stock	2 tablespoons chopped parsley
1 × 400 g (14 oz) can okra, drained or 225 g (8 oz) fresh okra, trimmed	

Preparation time: _20-25 minutes_
Cooking time: _about 1 hour_
Oven: _180°C, 350°F, Gas Mark 4_

Okra is an unusual ingredient which, as well as adding flavour and texture, is used as a thickening agent in casseroles and stews. When available, fresh okra gives better results and a good colour to this dish.

1. Heat the fat in a pan and fry the chicken pieces until golden brown. Transfer to a casserole.
2. Add the oil to the pan and fry the onion, garlic and green pepper for 2 minutes until soft.
3. Sprinkle on the flour, then add the tomatoes and stock and bring to the boil.
4. Slice the okra thickly and add to the pan with the tomato purée, Worcestershire sauce, cloves, chilli powder, basil, salt and pepper. Simmer gently for 5 minutes.
5. Pour over the chicken, cover the casserole and cook in a preheated oven for about 1 hour or until tender.
6. Adjust the seasoning and serve the gumbo on a bed of cooked rice, tossed with chopped fresh parsley.

Jambalaya

2 tablespoons oil	150 g (5 oz) long grain rice
25 g (1 oz) butter or margarine	450 ml (¾ pint) beef stock
450 g (1 lb) lean pork, cut into narrow strips	¼ teaspoon ground allspice
	salt
1 large onion, peeled and chopped	freshly ground black pepper
	100 g (4 oz) smoked sausage, sliced or chopped
1 green pepper, deseeded and sliced	100 g (4 oz) peeled prawns
	To garnish:
1 red pepper, deseeded and sliced	few whole prawns
	tomato wedges
100 g (4 oz) mushrooms, thickly sliced	

Preparation time: *20 minutes*
Cooking time: *1 hour*
Oven: *180°C, 350°F, Gas Mark 4*

1. Heat the oil and butter in a pan and fry the pieces of pork until well browned. Transfer to a large casserole.
2. Fry the onions gently in the same fat until soft. Add the peppers and continue cooking for 3-4 minutes, stirring frequently.
3. Add the mushrooms and continue cooking for a further 1 minute, then stir in the rice followed by the stock and bring to the boil.
4. Add the allspice, salt and pepper and the smoked sausage. Pour over the pork, mix well and cover tightly. Cook in a preheated oven for 45 minutes.
5. Stir well, add the prawns and a little more boiling stock if necessary. Cover again and return to the oven for about 15 minutes or until the liquid has been absorbed and the meat is tender.
6. Garnish with whole prawns and tomato wedges.

Jambalaya

Polish 'Nelson' steaks

4 rump steaks, about 175 g
(6 oz) each

40 g (1½ oz) seasoned flour

75 g (3 oz) butter or margarine

1 large onion, peeled and
sliced

175 g (6 oz) mushrooms, sliced

150 ml (¼ pint) single cream

150 ml (¼ pint) beef stock

salt

freshly ground black pepper

450 g (1 lb) potatoes, peeled
and cut into 2.5 cm (1 inch)
cubes

To garnish:
chopped fresh parsley
(optional)

cooked carrot sticks

Preparation time: *15 minutes*
Cooking time: *about 1 hour*
Oven: *180°C, 350°F, Gas Mark 4*

1. Coat the steaks in seasoned flour. Melt 50 g (2 oz) of the fat in a pan and fry the steaks to seal quickly on both sides. Transfer to the casserole.

2. Add the remaining fat to the pan and fry the onion until soft. Add the mushrooms and continue cooking for 1 minute.
3. Add the cream and stock to the pan and bring to the boil. Add salt and pepper and pour over the steaks.
4. Cover the casserole and cook in a preheated oven for 20 minutes.
5. Add the potatoes to the casserole, cover again and return to the oven for about 40 minutes or until the potatoes and steak are tender.
6. Serve the steaks with their sauce and vegetables in a deep serving dish, garnished with chopped parsley (if using) and carrot sticks.

LEFT TO RIGHT: Polish 'Nelson' steaks; Australian spiced lamb

Australian spiced lamb

Serves 4-6

½ teaspoon grated nutmeg	100 g (4 oz) soft brown sugar
½ teaspoon ground cinnamon	150 ml (¼ pint) wine vinegar
1.5-1.75 kg (3½ -4 lb) leg of lamb, boned	salt
	freshly ground black pepper
8 whole cloves	150 ml (¼ pint) water
1 large onion, peeled and sliced	1 tablespoon cornflour
	To garnish:
1 garlic clove, peeled and crushed	courgettes
	new potatoes

Preparation time: *20 minutes, plus overnight marinating*
Cooking time: *1½ -2 hours*
Oven: *180°C, 350°F, Gas Mark 4*

Your butcher should remove the bones from the lamb if you ask him in advance, otherwise provided you have a small sharp knife, it is quite simple to do. Work carefully round top bone to loosen it from the rest of the flesh, scraping off all the meat as you go. Remove the first bone and then continue to remove the lower bone. Tie the joint loosely into shape with string.

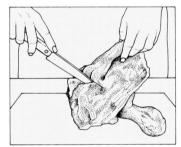
Loosen flesh from top bone.

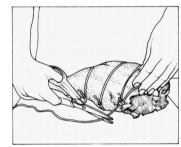
Scrape off meat; remove bone.

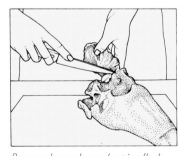
Remove lower bone, leaving flesh.

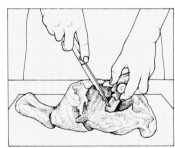
Remove end bone; tie with string.

1. Mix the nutmeg and cinnamon together and rub all over the lamb. Place in a large casserole.
2. Add the cloves, onion and garlic to the casserole, then blend the sugar, vinegar, salt, pepper and water together and pour over.
3. Cover the casserole tightly and leave in a cool place for 20-24 hours, turning the meat several times.

4. Next day, cover the casserole and cook in a preheated oven for 1½-2 hours or until tender, basting once.
5. Remove the lamb to a serving dish and keep warm,. Discard the cloves.
6. Spoon off any excess fat from the pan juices, blend the cornflour with a little cold water, add to the pan and bring to the boil. Boil rapidly, uncovered, for about 5 minutes to reduce a little. Adjust seasoning and serve with the lamb . Garnish with courgettes and potatoes.

Pollo cacciatore

1.75 kg (4 lb) chicken or 4 large chicken portions	1 teaspoon dried basil
	1 tablespoon tomato purée (optional)
3 tablespoons oil	
2 large onions, peeled and sliced	150 ml (¼ pint) red wine
	salt
2 garlic cloves, peeled and crushed	freshly ground black pepper
1 × 425 g (15 oz) can tomatoes	
2 tablespoons chopped fresh parsley or 1 tablespoon dried parsley	

Preparation time: *15 minutes*
Cooking time: *about 1 hour*
Oven: *160°C, 325°F, Gas Mark 3*

This is a traditional Italian recipe in which the chicken is flavoured with garlic, tomatoes and basil.

1. Cut the chicken into 8 pieces (or halve the portions) and remove the skin.
2. Heat the oil in a pan and fry the chicken pieces until browned all over. Transfer to a casserole.
3. Add the onions and garlic to the pan and fry until golden brown. Add the tomatoes with their juice, the parsley, basil, tomato purée [if using] and wine, then bring to the boil. Add salt and pepper to taste.
4. Pour the mixture over the chicken, cover the casserole and cook in a preheated oven for about 1 hour or until tender.
5. Adjust the seasoning and serve very hot with pasta.

Boeuf Bourguignon

675 g (1½ lb) topside of beef,
cut into 2.5 cm (1 inch) cubes
300 ml (½ pint) red wine
1 garlic clove, peeled and
crushed
1 bay leaf
2 tablespoons oil or dripping
175 g (6 oz) piece streaky
bacon, derinded and diced
12 button onions, peeled
1 tablespoon flour

150 ml (¼ pint) beef stock
salt
freshly ground black pepper
2-3 tablespoons brandy
100 g (4 oz) button mushrooms,
trimmed
To garnish:
fried bread triangles
chopped fresh parsley
(optional)

Preparation time: *20 minutes, plus marinating*
Cooking time: *2-2¼ hours*
Oven: *160°C, 325°F, Gas Mark 3*

1. Place the beef in a bowl with wine, garlic and bay leaf. Cover and leave to marinate for 3 hours.
2. Drain the beef, reserving the marinade, heat the oil or dripping in a pan and fry with the bacon, until well sealed. Transfer to a casserole.
3. Fry the onions in the same fat until lightly browned, then sprinkle in the flour and cook for 1 minute. Add the wine marinade and stock and bring to the boil; add salt and pepper to taste.
4. Warm the brandy, pour over the beef and ignite; then cover with the wine sauce.
5. Cover the casserole and cook in a preheated oven for 1½ hours.
6. Add the mushrooms, taste and adjust the seasoning and return to the oven for 30-45 minutes or until tender. Discard the bay leaf.
7. Serve garnished with fried bread triangles and chopped parsley (if using).

Variations:

Topside is the best cut of meat to use for this recipe, but to cut the cost, use braising or chuck steak. Allow 1 kg (2 lb) of either of these, trim to remove any fat and gristle, then cut into 2.5 cm (1 inch) cubes. Increase the cooking time to 2-2½ hours. After 1½ hours, check the liquid in the casserole and, if a little dry, add about 150 ml (¼ pint) boiling stock.

For a different flavour add 175 g (6 oz) no-need-to-soak prunes or 1 deseeded and sliced red pepper 1 hour before the end of cooking time. For a herby flavouring, add 2 tablespoons chopped fresh herbs or 1 tablespoon dried mixed herbs or any individual herb such as oregano, marjoram or basil.

Boston baked beans

350 g (12 oz) haricot beans,
soaked
450 g (1 lb) belly pork, skinned
2 large onions, peeled and
sliced
2 teaspoons salt
1½ teaspoons dry mustard
freshly ground black pepper

2 tablespoons black treacle
2 tablespoons wine vinegar
8 whole cloves
1 tablespoon tomato purée or
2 tablespoons tomato ketchup
chopped fresh parsley or mixed
fresh herbs, to garnish

Preparation time: *15 minutes, plus soaking*
Cooking time: *7 hours*
Oven: *150°C, 300°F, Gas Mark 2*

Boston baked beans are an American favourite and to do the recipe justice, long slow cooking is essential. First wash the beans thoroughly in cold water, then soak overnight in fresh cold water. An emergency method of soaking is to bring the unsoaked beans to the boil in fresh cold water for 10 minutes, then cover and leave to get cold. Rinse and use.

1. Drain the beans and place in a large heavy ovenproof casserole.
2. Trim the pork and cut into 2.5 cm (1 inch) pieces, discarding any pieces of gristle and bone.
3. Add the pork to the beans with the onions, salt, mustard, plenty of pepper, the treacle, vinegar, cloves and tomato purée or ketchup and mix well.
4. Add sufficient cold water to the casserole barely to cover the ingredients and cover tightly. If the lid is not a good fit, cover first with foil. Cook in a preheated oven for 6 hours.
5. Stir well, add a little boiling water if the contents are getting too dry and adjust the seasoning. Cover again and return to the oven for a further 1 hour.
6. Discard the cloves, if possible and serve sprinkled with chopped parsley or fresh herbs.

Variation:

Butter beans may be used in place of haricot beans; soak them in the same way before cooking.

Salted belly of pork or salted silverside may be used in place of fresh pork but reduce the salt by 1 teaspoon.

Italian pork balls

675g (1½ lb) raw minced pork
2 garlic cloves, peeled and crushed
½ teaspoon ground cinnamon
good pinch of ground cloves
salt
freshly ground black pepper
1 egg, beaten
25 g (1 oz) flour
3 tablespoons oil

1 large onion, peeled and chopped
1 red pepper, deseeded and sliced
6 tomatoes, peeled and sliced
1 tablespoon tomato purée
6 whole cloves
150 ml (¼ pint) red wine
1 tablespoon cornflour

Preparation time: *20 minutes*
Cooking time: *50-60 minutes*
Oven: *180°C, 350°F, Gas Mark 4*

1. Combine the pork, 1 garlic clove, cinnamon and cloves, season with salt and pepper. Add the egg to bind together, divide into 16 and shape into balls. Roll in the flour.

2. Heat the oil and fry the pork balls until lightly browned. Transfer to a casserole.
3. Fry the onion and remaining garlic in the same pan until soft. Add the pepper and continue cooking until the onions are lightly browned.
4. Add the tomatoes, tomato purée, cloves, wine and salt and pepper and pour over the pork balls.
5. Cover the casserole and cook in a preheated oven for 50-60 minutes or until tender.
6. Discard the cloves, skim and thicken the sauce with the cornflour blended in a little cold water. Bring back to the boil, adjust the seasoning and serve on a bed of pasta.

CLOCKWISE FROM THE LEFT: Italian pork balls; Boeuf Bourguignon; Boston baked beans

New England chicken

1.75 g (4 lb) chicken, cut into 8 pieces	1 × 225 gv (8 oz) can oysters, drained
salt	150 ml (¼ pint) double cream
freshly ground black pepper	2 teaspoons cornflour
50 g (2 oz) butter	¼ teaspoon dried basil
150 ml (¼ pint) milk	To garnish:
¼ teaspoon dried sage	watercress

Preparation time: *15 minutes*
Cooking time: *about 1¼ hours*
Oven: *180°C, 350°F, Gas Mark 4*

In New England oysters are very plentiful in the Fall. Here they are not so easy to come by and are very expensive; however canned oysters make a good alternative. Use 175 g (6 oz) shelled, drained fresh oysters.

1. Sprinkle the chicken with salt and pepper. Melt the butter in a pan and fry the pieces of chicken until golden. Transfer to a casserole with the butter.
2. Pour the milk over the chicken and sprinkle with salt, pepper and the sage.
3. Cover and cook in a preheated oven for 1 hour.
4. Uncover the casserole and add the oysters. Blend the cream with the cornflour and stir into the casserole with the basil. Cover again and return to the oven for 15-20 minutes to reheat thoroughly.
5. Serve garnished with watercress.

Australian curry hotpot

Serves 5-6

3 tablespoons oil or dripping	300 ml (½ pint) beef stock
1 kg (2 lb) braising steak, cut into 2.5 cm (1 inch) cubes	1 × 425 g (15 oz) can tomatoes
2 large onions, peeled and sliced	100 g (4 oz) raisins
	2 tablespoons wine vinegar
2 large cooking apples, peeled, cored and sliced	salt
	To garnish:
1 tablespoon curry powder	hard-boiled eggs, sliced
1 tablespoon flour	sprigs of parsley
	potato crisps

Preparation time: *15 minutes*
Cooking time: *about 2-2½ hours*
Oven: *180°C, 350°F, Gas Mark 4*

1. Heat the oil or dripping in a pan and fry the beef until brown. Transfer to a casserole.
2. Fry the onions in the same pan until soft, then add the apples and continue cooking for 2-3 minutes.
3. Sprinkle the curry powder and flour over the onions, mix well, then add the stock and bring to the boil.
4. Add the tomatoes, raisins, vinegar and salt and pour over the beef. Cover the casserole.
5. Cook in a preheated oven for 2 hours. Stir well, adjust the seasoning and if necessary return to the oven for 15-30 minutes or until the meat is very tender.
6. Serve in a fairly shallow dish with slices of egg down the centre, and sprigs of parsley and crisps around the edge of the dish.

CLOCKWISE FROM THE LEFT: New England chicken; Oxtail with black olives; Australian curry hotpot

Oxtail with black olives

Serves 6-8

2 oxtails, cut up	grated rind of ½ orange
3 tablespoons olive oil	juice of 1 orange
4 tablespoons brandy	600 ml (1 pint) beef stock
1 onion, peeled and sliced	225 g (8 oz) stoned black olives
1 garlic clove, peeled and crushed	50 g (2 oz) butter or margarine
	50 g (2 oz) flour
200 ml (7 fl oz) dry white wine	fresh parsley, to garnish
2 bay leaves	(optional)
salt	
freshly ground black pepper	

Preparation time: *about 20 minutes, plus chilling overnight*
Cooking time: *4½ hours*
Oven: *160°C, 325°F, Gas Mark 3*

1. Trim the oxtails of excess fat. Heat the oil in a pan and fry the meat until browned all over. Transfer to a casserole.
2. Warm the brandy, pour over the oxtail and ignite.
3. Fry the onion and garlic in the fat left in the pan until golden brown. Add the wine and bring to the boil.
4. Pour over the oxtail and add the bay leaves, salt and pepper, the orange rind and juice.
5. Bring the stock to the boil and add sufficient barely to cover the oxtail.
6. Cover the casserole and cook in a preheated oven for 3 hours.
7. Pour the liquid into a bowl and chill. Discard the bay leaves, cool and chill the oxtail overnight.
8. The next day, remove the layer of fat from the cooking liquid, bring back to the boil and pour over the oxtail; add the olives. Cover and cook for a further 1-1½ hours or until tender.
9. Cream the butter and flour together to make a beurre manié.
10. Strain off the juices and reserve 600 ml (1 pint). Whisk the beurre manié into the sauce, a little at a time, until thickened; bring back to the boil and adjust the seasoning.
11. Arrange the oxtail and olives in a serving dish and pour the sauce over. Garnish with parsley (if using).

Oxtail has a high proportion of bone and is generally rather fatty. The flavour, however, is excellent but it needs long slow cooking, it is thus ideal for casseroles and stews. Choose an oxtail with bright red flesh and creamy white fat. The butcher often sells oxtail ready cut up, so the colour will have dulled, and sometimes they are available frozen, when they must be thoroughly thawed before cooking. If cutting your own, use a sharp knife and a chopper or saw and cut into pieces about 5 cm (2 inches) thick; then trim off any excess fat.

INDEX